# THE ROMANOV DYNASTY
## GENEALOGICAL TABLE

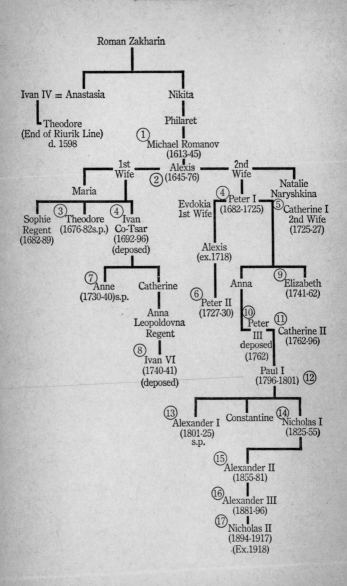

# RISE AND FALL
# OF THE ROMANOVS

ANATOLE G. MAZOUR

*Professor of History*
*Stanford University*

## AN ANVIL ORIGINAL

*under the general editorship of*

LOUIS L. SNYDER

D. VAN NOSTRAND COMPANY, INC.

PRINCETON, NEW JERSEY

TORONTO                                    LONDON

NEW YORK

TO JOSEPHINE—THE SOURCE OF INSPIRATION

D. VAN NOSTRAND COMPANY, INC.
120 Alexander St., Princeton, New Jersey (*Principal office*)
24 West 40 St., New York, N.Y.
25 Hollinger Rd., Toronto 16, Canada
358, Kensington High Street, London, W.14, England

Copyright © 1960, by
ANATOLE G. MAZOUR
Published simultaneously in Canada by
D. Van Nostrand Company (Canada), Ltd.

Library of Congress Catalog Card No. 60-13460

PRINTED IN THE UNITED STATES OF AMERICA

# PREFACE

The story of the three-century-old Romanov dynasty is so closely interwoven with the history of Russia that an account of one without the other hardly makes any sense. The "If" historian can be promised a fascinating time in taking up such hypothetical questions as these: How different would the course of Russian history have been had there never been a Peter the Great? What might have been the effect upon the course of western European history had Alexander I been willing to coöperate with Napoleon in enforcing the Continental Blockade? What would have been the fate of Austria had Nicholas I been a "neutralist" or "isolationist" in 1848? Whatever the answers to these endless questions might be, one thing becomes increasingly clear: regardless of the part the masses might play in history, their rulers are not to be dismissed as negligible historical factors. Strong or weak, active or apathetic, sovereigns in Russian history have left deep imprints upon the course of events and helped to shape the pattern of national life. Whether they accelerated expansion or preferred the *status quo*, whether they maintained peace or delivered war, they contributed more than their share to the shaping of national history. If the reader derives this conclusion, the author's effort in presenting this historical account is fully justified.

*Stanford University*          ANATOLE G. MAZOUR

# TABLE OF CONTENTS

# Part I

# THE ROMANOV DYNASTY

# — 1 —

# THE ROMANOV ASCENDANCY

**The Early Romanovs.** When Tsar Theodore I died in 1598, the last descendant of the Riurik dynasty passed into history. This resulted in a fifteen-year social and political upheaval commonly referred to as The Time of Troubles. The successor to the throne (in February, 1613) was a young lad by the name of Michael Romanov, who was destined to initiate the new dynastic line that lasted precisely 304 years. Who were the Romanovs and how did the family come to be chosen as the new dynasty?

The origin of the Romanov family is none too clear and is particularly complicated by the fact that during the early Muscovite period changing names was, for various reasons, a common practice. The earliest reference to what was destined to become the Romanov dynasty is to be found in the Chronicle under the date 6855, that is, 1346. The Chronicle reads:[1]

> In the summer of 6855 [1346]. . . . Grand Prince Semyon Ivanovich, grandson of Daniel, was married for the third time; he married Mary, the daughter of Grand Prince Alexander Mikhailovich of Tver; and those who went to Tver after her were Andrei Kobyla and Aleksei Besovolkov.[2]

Later the Chronicle has reference to another member of the family line under the name of Theodore Koshka, a prominent boyar and associate of the Grand Duke Dimitri Donskoi (1359-89). His sons changed the name to Koshkin and two sons of Zakhari Koshkin adopted the name of Zakharin-Koshkin and later Zakharin. The

---

[1] *Polnoye sobraniye russkikh lietopisei,* vol. X, 218.

[2] The name *Kobyla* appears in later years in various alternate forms, as *Kambila, Kabyla, Kabylin,* and *Kobylin.*

star of the Zakharins quickly ascended when Anastasia, the daughter of Roman, married Ivan IV, thereby raising the family to the highest ranks (an honor some families came to frown upon). Of the latter's descendants, one Nikita Romanovich Zakharin played a most prominent part at the time of Ivan IV. The patronymic name eventually became the name of the new Russian dynasty—Romanov.

**Rise to Eminence.** The road of the Romanovs to the throne was strewn not only with roses but sharp thorns as well. During the brief reign of Theodore I, the grandfather of Michael Romanov, Nikita, acting as regent, came to share the responsibilities with Boris Godunov. The death of Theodore and the ensuing dynastic crisis terminated their friendly coöperation and soon the two became bitter rivals for political power. There was good reason for Boris to suspect the conduct of the Romanovs, cautious though it might have been. The Romanovs were friendly with the False Pretenders and they enjoyed far more popularity in the country than Boris ever did. It was the First Pretender, better known as False Dimitri, who appointed the father of Michael Romanov to the bishopric of Rostov. Small wonder that shortly after Boris attained the throne the Romanovs became the target of severe attacks. One of the first things Boris did was compel Theodore Romanov (under the name of Philaret), and his wife Mary (as Martha), to take monastic vows. Michael thus became separated from his father in infancy. From about the middle of the reign of Ivan IV the masses regarded the Romanovs as a model boyar family who championed the cause of the people only to become victims of political persecution.

**Romanovs During the Time of Troubles.** If at the time of Ivan IV the Romanovs managed to hold aloof from politics, from the time of Boris they became seriously embroiled. With the ascendancy of Prince Shuisky (1606-10) things did not improve because the Romanovs had openly opposed him as a candidate to the throne. After four years Shuisky was overthrown: the candidacy of Ladislas, the son of the King of Poland, was advocated. In the midst of this struggle the Second False Pretender made his appearance. The internal conflicts resulting in foreign intervention and invasion led to the inevitable outcome—the rise of a national movement that rebelled against all foreign orientations and the establishment of order and peace by its own national forces. The movement was headed by a humble burgher from Nizhni-Novgorod, Kuzma Minin, and a nobleman, Prince Pozharsky. After their inspiring appeals to the people, the two leaders managed to form a national army that expelled the Polish invaders from Moscow. By October, 1612, Minin and Pozharsky had issued a call to elect deputies to a national assembly for the purpose of electing a new tsar and restoring peace and public order. The following February the deputies—perhaps one of the most representative assemblies ever gathered in Moscow —met to determine the future of Russia.

One of the first decisions they made was not to consider foreign candidates to the vacant throne. They thought it particularly undesirable to have a successor urged by the Polish king and backed by the Polish army, a choice which might occasion political and religious problems later. For this reason the church as well as others hailed the decision as a national triumph.

**Election to the Throne.** Having decided upon the selection of a native candidate the next problem was the naming of such a candidate. This proved a far more difficult task, since the preceding events had gravely thinned the ranks of the old titled aristocracy: those who survived the last half of the century of tyranny, error, and turmoil often compromised themselves either by collaboration with the Polish invaders, or by supporting other lost or suspect causes. Others who proved loyal during the trying years were not socially qualified to be considered for the establishment of the new dynasty. The Romanov family itself was not able to take an active part in the assembly: the father, Philaret, was a prisoner of war in Poland; a brother, Ivan, remained in Moscow during the occupation and was considered disqualified; Michael resided with his mother in a convent not far from Moscow. Other members of the Romanov family were scattered throughout the land. It was a family missing its head, lacking physical as well as political unity.

But in 1613 the national assembly thought of Michael Romanov for various reasons: the family's eminence, its unblemished record during the second half of the reign of Ivan IV, the popularity of certain of its members among the people represented at the assembly, and above all the fact of the matrimonial tie with the royal family. By considering Michael Romanov, a first cousin once removed of the last tsar, Theodore I, the assembly believed that genealogical continuity was confirmed. (Theodore I was the son of Anastasia, a sister of Nikita Romanov, the grandfather of Michael.) The Romanovs were wise enough to remain aloof from the tyrannical administration of Ivan IV, and so succeeded in cultivating popularity and later gaining respect. The masses considered Michael's grandfather, Nikita Romanov, as their champion. The candidate's father, Theodore (known better by his church name of Philaret), was a noted scholar of his day.

"Dynastic Continuity." Because of his high church office it was considered improper to offer Theodore the crown; his son Michael, therefore, was the logical candidate. Furthermore, in the absence of the father the young boy might be willing to follow the counsel of the assembly. Such was the feeling of the majority of deputies, who represented the burghers, the free peasantry, the Cossacks, the higher and lower clergy, and the greater and lesser nobility. After much debate only the greater nobility and the peasantry manifested some hesitance, while the lesser nobility, the Cossacks, and the burghers unconditionally supported the Romanov candidate. The assembly, being generally conservative, felt that it would have been politically unwise to introduce a totally new dynasty; on the contrary, it sought to give the impression that the disruption of the dynastic line was accidental and its restoration a natural act. Michael Romanov thus served as a symbol not only of legitimacy, but also of dynastic continuity. In essence the assembly sanctioned what Ivan IV had been aiming at with such fury: an absolute monarchy in which the new tenant landlords or lesser nobility, the burgher class, and the Cossacks constituted the backbone of the state. (*See Reading No. 1.*)

Michael Romanov ascended the throne as hereditary sovereign of the Russian state, bearing the crown by divine right. The former concept of the state as a hereditary patrimony henceforth became invalidated by the new status of the crown. The Boyar Council shared the same fate: doomed by the nature of the resurrected state to political oblivion. Furthermore, upon the return from Poland of Michael's father, an illustrious figure was added to the high ranks of government. In June, 1619, in the presence of the Patriarch of Jerusalem, Philaret was consecrated as Patriarch of Russia. From that date on until his death in 1633, Patriarch Philaret played a prominent part not only as head of the church, but as a distinguished leader of the state as well. The country was virtually governed by both the father and the son. Secular and spiritual powers seemed to have merged into a single source of authority. Years of harsh experience had hardened Patriarch Philaret and turned him into a determined despot with a touch of bitterness as well as an aura of parochialism. Yet whatever one might say of Patriarch Philaret, the Romanov's early success was largely due to him.

— 2 —

# THE REIGN OF MICHAEL ROMANOV, 1613-45

**The First Romanov.** The legacy inherited by the new Romanov dynasty was a sorrowful one. The fifteen-year Time of Troubles left the state economically exhausted, socially restless, financially bankrupt, militarily insecure. Conditions cried for a great leader, which Michael was not; neither his age nor his physical condition suited him for the task that lay ahead. He came to the throne at the age of sixteen, while his father was still in Poland. In Philaret's absence, and while the young tsar was gaining knowledge and experience, the real authority remained in the hands of a council. The national emergency also necessitated that the council be aided by the general assembly, which assumed an important place in government and was frequently consulted on national issues. The assembly included deputies from the nobility, the clergy, the townsmen, and the free peasantry. During the first nine years of Michael's reign the assembly was virtually in continuous session. Later it was summoned on three other occasions, in 1632, 1637, and 1642. As the monarchy gained strength the assembly began to decline, meeting only five times in the eight years between 1645-53, after which its authority began to fade and finally vanished altogether: the more secure the administration's position, the more superfluous was the assembly. Its greatest service—one which, strangely enough, led to its own obliteration—was the promulgation of the Code of Laws finally adopted in 1648-49.

**Internal Problems.** From the moment of his Patriarchy (1619) until his death in 1633, Philaret handled both church and state affairs with a steady hand. Signs of the oncoming crisis were already present, but while both state and church issues were directed by the same person there was obviously less likelihood of conflict. After Philaret's death, relations worsened between temporal and ecclesiastical authorities.

**Financial Difficulties.** Perhaps the country's most acute problem, one that caused much concern, was the sorrowful state of its finances after 1613, when the old system of taxation broke down. Formerly the state taxed land under cultivation; considerable reduction of that area during the Time of Troubles spelled disaster for the production level as well as for the source of revenue. Aside from the serious deficits that the state had to face, whatever revenue it did collect was wastefully administered. Widespread abuses throughout the country urgently required a tightening of discipline and the riddance of many despotic local officials who arbitrarily set up their own rules and regulations. The system needed overhauling to provide an individual tax and new methods of land assessment, for the obsolete system of taxing cultivated areas only lent itself to numerous evasions. The administration needed to take stock of the taxable population and to check the migratory tendencies of those who eluded their anchorage and evaded financial responsibilities. On the other hand, many protested that their tax

burdens were crushingly heavy and entirely dispropor-
tionate to their ability to pay. In its efforts to restore
public order the state resorted to measures which led to
the establishment of serfdom, the implications of which
can hardly be overestimated.

**External Problems.** Foreign affairs were equally
complex, involving relations with Poland and Sweden,
whose armies had recently invaded and now held parts
of Russian territory. It took great sacrifices to wrench
back from Poland such strategically important positions
as Smolensk, Seversk, and later the southern areas. And
while Moscow was preoccupied with Poland, Sweden
invaded the Novgorod area (which not even the national
upsurge of 1612 was able to liberate), thereby blocking
Moscow's precarious outlet to the Baltic Sea.

But the Polish problem was considered the most vital,
for the traditional rival held under its control large territories considered Russian from the Kievan period. The
conflict was sharpened further by what Moscow regarded
as forced subversion of faithful Greek Orthodox communities by cunning devices such as the formation of the
Uniate church, which tolerated Orthodox ritual but required allegiance to Rome. Memories were still too fresh
of Poland's support of impostors such as the First and
the Second Dimitris, who pretended to be the killed youthful Dimitri and lawful claimant to the throne. It was the
Polish army that invaded and burned Moscow, blocked
all roads to the sea, and cooperated with the Crimean
Tartars against Russian aspirations in the south and southwest. Finally, it was the Polish government that refused
to recognize the recently elected Romanov dynasty and
for many years maintained the right of Ladislas to the
throne of Russia. Peace with Poland, though advisable,
was difficult to achieve because of charges and counter-
charges accumulated over a century.

Yet because of internal weakness Moscow could only
wait for more favorable opportunities. The grim fact
remained that Poland was formidable while Russia, helpless and enervated by her recent experiences, was in no
position to reclaim either her injured prestige nor her
lost territories. Any attempt at reclaiming Great, Little,
and White Russians in the southwest and west would
invariably have provoked a conflict with Poland, while

a struggle for commercial and military control over the shores of the Baltic would undoubtedly have led to war with either Poland or Sweden or both. Finally, any attempt to reach the Black Sea would have meant war with Turkey, probably supported by Poland. Thus, for the immediate future Moscow had to think in terms of survival rather than of fulfilling national aspirations.

With Sweden Moscow succeeded in concluding the Treaty of Stolbovo in 1617, a document which only confirmed Russia's weak position against her two hostile neighbors. Russia had to concede the loss of Oreshek (or Nöteborg), Yamburg, and part of Carelia, including Keksholm—all strategically important areas. All that could be said of the treaty was that it secured temporarily a measure of peace. Any effort to dislodge the Poles, however, and recover Smolensk and Seversk was blocked by Russia's inferior military power as well as by the fact that Ladislas continued to claim his right to the throne. The brief negotiations broke down and in 1618 war again flared up. After initial successes, the Polish army was held at Tushino, in a stalemate which, as each side realized, might sap the strength of either army. The opponents consented to open negotiations once more and met at the Trinity monastery, outside of Moscow, where they reached a truce agreement that lasted exactly fourteen-and-a-half years. The two governments agreed to exchange prisoners of war, among whom, incidentally, was Metropolitan Philaret. Poland retained Smolensk and Seversk and Ladislas still maintained his claims.

In 1632 the war between Poland and Russia broke out anew. Sigismund III died and was succeeded by Ladislas. The Russian army opened a successful offensive, but at Smolensk it was stopped cold. Here neither side could make further progress, and by 1634 both contestants evidently having had enough of war, decided to sign a treaty of peace. Ladislas renounced his claim to the throne of Russia and recognized Michael as lawful tsar. But still Poland kept Smolensk and Seversk. Completely exhausted by recent civil strife and bled from without by continuous warfare, Russia had to have peace at any cost. To what degree the country was enfeebled may be judged by the following incident. In 1637 the Don Cossacks seized Azov and appealed to the Tsar for aid. Tsar Michael quickly summoned the national assembly for counsel. After much deliberation the assembly turned the offer down for the simple reason that Moscow was financially unable either to aid the Cossacks or to face the prospect of war with Turkey over the matter. And so, to their great embarrassment, the Cossacks were forced to relinquish the rich prize they had won in unequal combat.

— 3 —

# THE REIGN OF ALEXIS, 1645-76

**Personality.** When Michael died in July, 1645, the assembly chose his only son, the sixteen-year-old Alexis. As in 1613, the assembly was guided by the genealogical line of the Romanov family. It is equally worth noting that after 1645 the election of each successor became virtually automatic: the primogeniture principle adhered to since the fourteenth century continued to be effective, and by the end of the seventeenth century the national assembly had died a natural death.

Alexis was noted for neither physical nor mental strength. Whereas Michael had been assisted by his able father, Patriarch Philaret, who for fifteen years was in charge of both temporal and ecclesiastical affairs, Alexis had no one behind him but his tutor, Boris I. Morozov. It was Morozov who decided whom Alexis was to marry: his choice, coinciding with the Tsar's, was the daughter of the prominent Vsevolzhsky family of the house of Miloslavsky. Shortly after Alexis was married Morozov himself became engaged to the sister of the Tsarina, which caused rumors in the capital concerning his limitless ambitions. For a while the Miloslavsky family wielded considerable power and simultaneously acquired notoriety for its corrupting influence. At this time certain groups with vested economic interests began effectively to reassert themselves. (*See Reading No. 2.*)

In June, 1648, administrative abuses accompanied by constantly increasing taxes provoked a violent mass uprising in Moscow. Under pressure of popular demand Alexis was forced to yield. One of the high officials, L. Pleshcheev, was seized and lynched by a mob while he was being led to the place of execution; another, P. Trakhaniotov, was executed; while Morozov himself was ordered to leave the capital. The repercussions of the popular uprising were felt for sometime to come. There were uprisings elsewhere: as late as 1650 a serious rebellion occurred in Novgorod, followed by one in Pskov. Thus, while the government was laboring over a new Code of Laws, the social order was continually challenged and for reason rules affecting the peasantry were tightened.

The historian of this period is in possession of two valuable eyewitness accounts which shed light on the character of Alexis as well as upon the general nature of his reign. Adam Olearius, head of the Schleswig-Holstein mission to Moscow, left a valuable description of life in Russia during the middle of the seventeenth century. Grigori Kotoshikhin, a minor government official in Moscow who defected to Stockholm, wrote there a unique narrative on conditions in his country at the time of Alexis. Both writers picture the ruler as acceptable to the electors in 1645 primarily because of his weakness of character.

At the age of five the boy was entrusted to his tutor, the aforementioned Boris I. Morozov, who taught him to read the Bible; at the age of nine he learned to sing church songs. This was about the entire "curriculum" of the Tsar. The toys of Alexis that are preserved in the museum cast some light upon his upbringing. These are soldiers, horses, armor, musical instruments, miniature wagons, horse sleighs, and a tiny library.

Ascending the throne at the age of sixteen the boy hardly knew what a carefree youth was. Small wonder that his tutor assumed the same role which his grandfather had at the time of Michael's ascendancy. But Morozov's assistance ended in 1648, and thereafter Alexis was thrown on his own resources and limited experience. During the years 1654-55, the young Tsar visited the front near Smolensk and Vilna, where for the first time he witnessed scenes of war and experienced the consequences of military defeat. At Riga he personally witnessed the military fiasco which left a deep impression upon him.

All his life Alexis remained a shy person, somewhat meek, his small deeply set eyes reflecting a kind nature. Even the political emigré Kotoshikhin, who was by no means friendly to the Moscow regime, ascribed political failure largely to the kindly meekness of Alexis. Though Alexis lacked an adequate education he always hoped to write. He left a number of verses of dubious poetic quality; he composed instructions for falconers, wrote memoirs about the Polish war, and loved to draft state documents. He was fond of philosophizing regardless of the subject and enjoyed expressing himself in rhetorical manner. He demonstrated an enthusiastic interest in a multitude of fields—politics, religion, military affairs, falconry, the problem of alcohol, the art of gardening, monastic life, theatrical art.

Though by nature tender, sensitive, and kindly in disposition, nonetheless he would succumb occasionally to outbursts of uncontrollable anger, especially on matters of religious or political principle. On such occasions he would scold the person involved, shout, and even display a readiness to engage in fights; he would use abusive language, call the offender a heathen, traitor, a "friend of the devil," or "son of Satan." At times he would scold and kick his father-in-law, Miloslavsky, and forcibly evict him from the chamber, though later he would repent and humbly beg forgiveness or send the old man gifts.

Alexis was an avid reader of religious and secular literature and often incorporated whole sentences from his reading into his own florid literary works. By nature Alexis was extremely pious, prayed and fasted frequently, and loved to discuss the subject of salvation. Religion to him was much more than lifeless dogma; his contemplative nature barred his faith from turning into a set of rigid rules. His religious belief was more a philosophical attitude toward life and a source of moral guidance, although his orthodoxy did not prevent him from admiring the stage and enjoying plays performed by Lutheran German actors. The theater he considered a useful and enlightening institution as well as an agency for entertainment.

National Issues. If the personality of the Tsar was rather a colorless one the same could not be said about the time of his reign; in some respects the reign of Alexis is associated with the most eventful developments of the century. The three decades are noted also for the disastrous mass uprisings provoked by general economic conditions. The perilous state of affairs compelled the recently established monarchy to employ all available means to stabilize the social order. The government hastened to initiate army reforms and supported church reforms which led to the Great Schism. The administration, supported by the nobility, sought measures to check the mobility of the roaming peasantry. These measures soon began to crystallize into institutionalized forms of serfdom. Along with it came the entrenchment of the landholding, serf-claiming nobility, now reassured of its privileged status but portentous of social and economic evils ahead.

Judicial Reforms. To consolidate the state further and to strengthen the shaken social frame the government set out to codify the laws of the land, a task it had neglected for over a century. By some quirk of fate in the summer of 1648, shortly before the general assembly had met to consider codification, riots broke out in Moscow and throughout the country. The effect upon the gathered deputies was instantaneous, frightened as they were by the specter of renewed civil war (memories of the recent Time of Troubles were still fresh). The assembly gathered in September, 1648, and quickly set up a commission to start revamping the code. The work proceeded with extraordinary speed and by the beginning of 1649 the commission managed to complete the assignment. The haste was largely caused by an eagerness to be ready for any national emergency; the government was willing to risk thoroughness in order to gain time and ability to cope with the acute situation. The new Code (*Sobornoye ulozheniye*) went immediately into effect and remained virtually unaltered until 1833.

Despite all precautions and the speed with which the new Code was adopted, revolt continued to flare up throughout the country. The uprisings that began in 1648

lasted for nearly two years. The country had hardly
recovered from these when in 1662 Moscow revolted at
revelations of serious fiscal abuses by the administration,
including members of the royal family. The uprising was
quelled only after costly military force was summoned.
Hardly had the latest unrest ended when a much graver
uprising occurred under the leadership of Stenka Razin.
The revolt began in the south among the Don Cossacks
and rapidly spread northward, reaching out as far as
Nizhni Novgorod. It took four years (1667-71) before
the government managed to liquidate the Razin rebellion.

**Early Western Influence.** During the reign of Alexis
various individuals came to the painful realization that
Russia needed to learn much from the West. They challenged native ossification and the deceptive sense of native superiority or smug security and recognized more
keenly Russia's backwardness. A belief in the infallibility
of Russia's old cultural and religious values came under
serious scrutiny. During the first half of the seventeenth
century western influence only trickled into Russia; during
the second half it began to seep irregularly through every
crevice; by the end of that century it was forced to flow
freely by order of Peter I himself. This influence and
thought came through devious channels—at first by way
of the need for superior western arms, and subsequently
through the invitation of engineers and artists. Later on,
in observing the foreign colony, the upper classes demanded foreign clothes, furniture, and theatrical produc-
tions, desired to study languages, and in general hoped
for a different way of life. Men like B. Morozov, Ordin
Nashchokin, A. S. Matveyev, or M. Rtishchev—all with
strong western proclivities and occupying at various times
important positions in the government—served as har-
bingers of the forthcoming century and of the coming
Peter I onto the scene of Russian history.

**The Religious Issue.** There were many lay and ecclesiastic leaders who were less receptive to the increased
influence of western culture. They frowned upon the study
of Latin and even Greek and were inimical to any pro-
western leniencies, regarding these as an inducement to
heresy. This sentiment was no more than passive until
the middle of the seventeenth century, when Patriarch
Nikon assumed office and set out to revise the liturgical

books of the church. With the tacit approval of the state
he began by correcting textual errors in the sacred books.
This action immediately provoked a storm of protests
and was interpreted by opponents as a heretical innovation. In vain did Nikon refer to original Greek texts to
justify his views. To resort to Greek texts as final authority at a time when the church in the Near East had been
lingering in Turkish captivity because, as the dissidents
argued, of its adoption of heretical teachings, was nothing
short of an insult to the faith. With fanatical dogmatism
the enemies of Nikon interpreted his policy as nothing
less than an effort to debase the purity of the faith so
carefully preserved by Russian orthodoxy. They cited as
an illustration the Council of Florence in 1439 and its
resolutions which the Greek church had accepted but
Moscow vehemently turned down. Fourteen years later
the mother church paid dearly for that folly when
in 1453 Constantinople fell into the hands of the infidel.
Since that time only the church of Moscow remained the
torch bearer of the pure faith. Since 1589 Russia had
created her own patriarchate and all along there was a
sense of spiritual superiority to any other church or ecclesiastic authority. How then, the opponents asked indig-
nantly, could Nikon refer to those foreign sources as
evidence of the true faith?

Patriarch Nikon. The revolt within the church was
connected with external developments. Nikon came to the
office of Patriarchate in 1652, at the time when the
reactivated struggle with Poland assumed a political as
well as a religious nature. To be able successfully to
challenge theological dogma the orthodox church had to
go to the original sources, which in this case meant By-
zantine sources, to Greek rituals, textual evidence, and
general writings, and on many occasions to Latin texts.
To those who had long come to accept the infallibility
of orthodoxy this seemed an inexplicable, unpardonable
sin; to them Nikon represented nothing less than the
devil incarnate. Yet Nikon was not a man to quail before
opponents nor to be intimidated by name-calling; he went
ahead with his plans regardless of rising hostility, and so
brought about the Great Schism within the church. From
the very beginning it was an uphill struggle, one that
culminated in 1667 with the excommunication of all

opponents of Nikon's reforms (better known as the Old Believers) and their leader, the Archpriest Avvakum.

Although Nikon won, he came to a sorrowful end himself. The reforms implied a dual struggle: ecclesiastical authority, which Nikon won, and political authority, which he lost. Because of the latter defeat Nikon eventually lost the influence he exercised over Tsar Alexis and in the end lost his office as well. The political defeat of Nikon had serious implications since the loss of ecclesiastic prestige proportionately increased the prestige of the sovereign. The opposition to the West was equally weakened and henceforth the church, though often displeased, was incapable of checking western influence upon Russian society.

Much took place during the reign of Alexis in the field of external affairs. Throughout the entire period attention was given predominantly to the question of Poland. At first it concerned mainly boundary problems, involving the areas of Smolensk and Seversk. Later the issues at stake assumed a much broader and far more complex character, concerning the entire south and southwestern areas including Kiev and the Ukrainian territory. The last issue became of grave concern when a mass uprising against Poland took place in 1654 and its leaders appealed to Moscow for aid. The case was further complicated by the Ottoman Empire's interest in the southern area.

Russo-Polish Relations. The basis for the social revolt was as complex as it was varied, involving economic, social, military, and religious problems. Tension had been accumulating ever since the death of Sigismund II Augustus (1548-72), marking the end of religious tolerance and the rise of fear of religious persecution among the orthodox population. To this must be added the serious political problem of Polish-Lithuanian unity. Did the union rest merely on an established dynastic tie or was it the basis of an indissoluble pact? It concerned further the status of the southern Cossacks, who rebelled against the persistent encroachment of Polish landlords and their continually extending serfdom. The delicate religious question was settled at the Congress of Brest-Litovsk in 1596, at which a portion of the Orthodox nobility and higher clergy consented to accept papal authority and conform the rites of the Orthodox to the Catholic church, though retaining the use of Slavonic in the service. The majority of the low clergy and the peasantry remained loyal to the Orthodox church and refused to join the newly formed "Uniate Church."

Through the years a number of parties had formed. Their programs and interests were varied, but they were bound by a common hatred of the domineering Pole, the "heretical" priest, and the exploiter landlord with his middleman Jew. During the first half of the seventeenth century revolts increasingly occurred, and each was quelled with greater harshness. Finally, in 1648, the revolt led by Bogdan Khmelnitsky assumed the proportions of a mass uprising. Pressed hard, yet determined against their enemy, the rebels appealed to their Orthodox brethren of Moscow for aid. Tempting as the call was it was not easy for Moscow to render assistance at once. The country had barely recovered from the preceding wars that had terminated in 1634, and the government was neither prepared nor willing to renew the conflict. Yet there was at the same time a popular feeling that if this opportunity were missed the Cossacks in desperation might turn to Turkey for assistance, or—what was worse—might be completely crushed by Poland. The result would be an even tighter Polish grip upon the Ukrainian people with no favorable solution in the foreseeable future. It must also be stated that the policy of Moscow and the aspirations of the Cossacks were not always harmonious. Yet when the decisive hour came the differences seemed inconsequential as compared with the magnitude of the issues at stake. The Cossacks sought protection under the Tsar and political autonomy; Moscow aimed eventually to establish absolute control over the southern territory. Both sides, while negotiating, engaged in cajolery before reaching agreement for common action.

After a period of hesitancy, Moscow came to the decision that it was unable to leave the Cossacks at the mercy of Poland and in 1654 joined the struggle. Russia was indirectly aided by Sweden, who during the same year declared war on Poland, thereby forcing upon Poland a formidable combination of forces. After two years Poland had no choice but to yield and by the Treaty of

Vilna in 1656 Moscow gained the Ukraine and White Russia. Encouraged by this victory the Russian government decided to gain control over the Baltic, thereby joining Sweden at war. The new turn of events saved Poland from total disaster and proved costly to Moscow. Khmelnitsky, meanwhile fearing, perhaps with good reason, that Russia and Poland might come to an agreement at the expense of the Ukraine, sought extra assurance by flirting with the Khan of Crimea and with Sweden. He did not live long enough to see the final outcome since he died in 1657; two years later the Cossacks in alliance with the Tartars defeated the Russians.

Taking advantage of this situation, Poland denounced the Treaty of Vilna, hastily concluded peace with Sweden, and renewed the war against Moscow in 1660. Anticipating the worst, Russia soon sued for peace with Sweden. According to the latest treaty stipulations Russia was completely barred from both the Gulf of Finland and the Baltic. Having concluded peace with Sweden, Russia still had to face a belligerent Poland. The protracted war had exhausted both. The ravaged southern part, now leaderless, where the two had fought, was divided as to which side to support. The Cossacks of the west bank of the Dnieper leaned toward Poland; the eastern bank favored loyalty to the Tsar of Moscow. The southern part, which suffered most severely, in despair sought protection from Turkey. It was in these circumstances that Poland and Russia decided to find means for a peaceful settlement.

**"The Permanent Peace" of Andrusovo, 1667.** In 1667, representatives of Poland and Russia met at Andrusovo, a small community southwest of Smolensk, where they signed a treaty of peace. In accordance with its provisions Russia regained the areas of Smolensk and Seversk as well as the territory east of the Dnieper, including the city of Kiev. Although in size the territorial gains did not seem commensurate with the enormous sacrifices of Moscow, nonetheless they proved important. For the time being the two states had had enough war and quickly accepted the terms of what hopefully came to be known as the "Permanent Peace" of Andrusovo.

**The Aftermath.** Henceforth Russo-Polish relations entered a new phase. The date 1667 came to be considered as the real beginning of the decline of Poland while

Russia ascended as the coming power in Eastern Europe. Neither side was particularly overjoyed by the peace terms, since both had drained their national resources and left behind them in the south an area entirely devastated by the long struggle. Since this was the first territorial expansion of any note under the Romanov dynasty the treaty was regarded as symbolic of a forthcoming consolidation of political power. But the newly gained territory posed new problems, the most significant of which concerned the Ottoman Empire: the conflict between the Cross and the Crescent, presumably for the emancipation of the Christian minorities, with forebodings of all the complexities of the present "Near Eastern Question." Another noteworthy development since 1667 was the virtual end of Russian isolationism; contacts with European countries assumed a normal and permanent basis. The chief diplomatic architect of this new development was Ordin Nashchokin, a truly modern statesman in Russia's rapid rise to power and the logical predecessor of Peter I. The regained Kievan area and the new western orientation may be regarded as the most outstanding achievements of the otherwise weak Tsar Alexis.

**Problem of Succession.** Tsar Alexis was married twice. Of the sixteen children he fathered, eleven daughters and two sons, Theodore, born in 1662, and Ivan, born in 1666, were by his first wife; by his second wife he had one son, Peter, born in 1672, and two daughters. In September, 1674, Alexis rather casually willed that Theodore become his successor and within less than two years the Tsar died at the early age of forty-six. The naming of a successor hardly solved the political problem since Theodore was only fourteen years of age and physically a very weak lad. To complicate matters further, in the spring of 1682 Theodore, then hardly twenty, died: in the absence of a law of succession the entire problem became momentous.

The confusion emanated largely from Alexis' marital entanglements. The Miloslavsky family of his first wife, and the Naryshkin family of his second, each had its relatives and each aspired to play a primary part at court. It should be noted as a detail that thus far the Romanov successors all reached the throne at a tender age, and were guided largely by their relatives or tutors during

the first years of their respective reigns. Later it became
extremely difficult to rid the government of the early
influences. The situation was bound to result in endless
intrigues, favoritism, plotting, and counterplotting. In the
case of Alexis' two marriages this was even more distress-
ing: the struggle between the Miloslavsky and Naryshkin
families became tense from the very start.

   **Theodore and Ivan.** At first the Naryshkins lost out,
the Tsarina being no match for the experienced intriguers
of the Miloslavskys. Under some flimsy pretext her two
brothers were banished from the capital and the Tsarina
herself was alienated from the Tsar. One of the most
ambitious and energetic members of the Miloslavsky
family was Sophie, sister of Theodore. It might be
noted that the Romanov females were usually physically
stronger than the males. The two surviving sons of the
first marriage, Theodore and Ivan, were both sickly boys.
Ivan's vision was impaired and he was mentally as well
as physically underdeveloped. Theodore was a dropsical
youth, who in addition also suffered from scurvy. Both
Theodore and Ivan, at the request of their father, studied
Latin and Polish. Their tutor, Simeon Polotsky, an extremely enlightened person for his time, performed as
good a job as he could. Aside from tutoring, Polotsky
also served as stage manager, councillor on ecclesiastical
matters, and composer of verses. It was Polotsky who
imbued Theodore with such pro-southern sentiments that
the boy wore a national Ukrainian costume. This in part
explained the rumors often heard in Muscovite circles
that labeled Polotsky a Polonophile and a "Uniate." The
belief was popularized when Theodore banned all Greek
missionaries from Russia.

   In 1680 Theodore married the daughter of a Polish
nobleman of Smolensk, Grushetski, which added fuel
to the fires of rumor. It was under the influence of his
Polish wife that Theodore, even prior to the ascendancy
of Peter, urged his people to shave their beards, alter
their national costumes, and don western style clothes;
he planned the introduction of a western system of education and suggested that Roman Catholic schools be
permitted. On the other hand, while these measures
strongly indicated pro-western tendencies and provoked
resentment and opposition in Russia, there was also

greater hope than ever in Poland that this might lead to
Russia's joining of the western church. There was no
justification for either rumor; nevertheless, it indicated
the prevailing atmosphere during the third quarter of
the seventeenth century.

Within a year after Theodore's marriage Tsarina Agafia
died in childbirth, while the newborn son died a few days
after his mother. Theodore remarried in February, 1682,
but within less than two months died himself, leaving
behind him two heirs, both with equal claims upon the
throne. Theodore at least inherited the throne by the
will of his father and had not been challenged. The heirs
who followed Theodore, Ivan and Peter, were less fortunate. Aside from the problem of legitimacy there were
questions of a different nature: Ivan was mentally feeble,
and his younger half-brother Peter was a minor. It was
this particular aspect of the issue that really caused the
dynastic crisis. The National Assembly had gone into
oblivion during the last few decades and the question of
summoning that body was not even raised. It was for
this reason that the Miloslavskys and Naryshkins emerged
as rivals for power.

**Miloslavsky vs. Naryshkin.** At first it seemed that
the Naryshkins were gaining control, but things soon
took a different course. In Moscow were quartered the
special regiments known as the Streltsy (Musketeers) or
Pretorian Guard, among whom was much unrest. Among
these troops were a predominant number of Old Believers,
who came mostly from either the more prosperous peasantry of Moscow's environs or from the middle class of
townspeople. The presence of these troops constituted a
threat for two reasons: they were well armed, and most
of them were literate and closely followed political developments at court. In due course the Streltsy were joined
by other malcontents: deserting serfs, Cossacks, and other
"sauntering" people, as these were called.

When Theodore died the Streltsy took advantage of
the occasion to press their own grievances, which in turn
offered opportunity to those who supported the candidacy
of Ivan for reasons of their own. In May the Streltsy
appeared in the Kremlin armed to demand the surrender
of all "traitors." When this was refused they broke into
the palace, caught many of the courtiers, and summarily

executed them. Among the victims were several members of the Naryshkin family, who perished under most brutal circumstances. It was in the midst of these hideous excesses that Sophie, assisted by the rebels, appeared on the scene.

From the start the Streltsy had favored Ivan as the next tsar, and after their successful uprising in May insisted upon his ascendancy. This created a most difficult problem. To add a stamp of legitimacy to the conflicting claims, the Patriarch and the still lingering Boyar Duma agreed to summon a general assembly that might sanction the choice. The assembly favored the candidacy of Peter, but they underestimated Sophie, who was determined not to be discounted in whatever decision was to be made. She was supported by the Streltsy and came to regard the decision of the assembly as nothing but the result of a family plot. Not wishing to aggravate the issue and cause a more serious crisis the delegates at last reached an unprecedented compromise: with the wisdom of Solomon it was ruled that both Ivan and Peter were to occupy the throne simultaneously while Sophie would serve as regent.

**Sophie as Regent.** How Sophie succeeded in gaining political prominence has been variously explained. No doubt it was due in part to her personal character: she possessed a strong will and a limitless thirst for power, and was ready to play any part in order to gain the throne. Since the Streltsy favored her candidacy she gladly accepted their assistance. Her skill at intrigue could rarely be matched and she was keenly intuitive of any political advantage. She was as unscrupulous, as one contemporary referred to her, as a Machiavellian without ever reading Machiavelli. As an associate of some of the younger men who represented new tendencies and orientations, Sophie utilized whatever information she could gain from them to advance her own interests. That she utilized the uprising of the Streltsy in an underhanded way has never been denied, although she played her part so slyly that there is only circumstantial evidence against her. The fact was that Sophie did not have to participate directly since her agents did all that was necessary to advance her candidacy.

In due course Sophie had good reason to lose faith in the loyalty of the Streltsy; the government contem-

plated a number of disciplinary measures and the more
demoralized units were ordered to the frontiers for guard
duty. It was Peter, however, who was destined much later
to settle the problem of the ever-restless Streltsy in the
capital. Meanwhile, as a minor, he watched helplessly
the ravages of these troops and his politically ambitious
half-sister exercising power while chaotic conditions continued. There was justified fear that when Peter came of
age he would revenge himself for his own agonizing experience as well as that of his mother and members of
his family, the Naryshkins. For the time being he resided
outside of Moscow, though always on the alert and ready
to return. Rumors reached him that with the aid of some
of her favorites Sophie schemed to be crowned as full
sovereign of Russia while the Patriarch and other supporters of Peter were to be banished.

Sophie shrewdly contemplated the consolidation of her
position by means of external successes. By signing an
alliance with Poland against Turkey she hoped to win a
great victory in the south. But while Peter was indig-
nantly following the events, the campaign against the
Crimea proved a sad failure. Relations between Sophie
and the Naryshkin family constantly worsened. In September, 1682, Peter informed his brother Ivan that the
time had arrived when the two should assume power;
that "disgraceful person," Sophie, was forced to retire
to a convent. Thereafter they shared the throne until the
end of 1696, when Ivan died and Peter alone assumed
the rule of Russia.

# — 4 —

# THE REIGN OF PETER I, 1682-1725

**Childhood.** We must now turn our attention to Peter. Born in 1672, he was the eldest child of Tsar Alexis' second marriage. At the age of four his father died and he remained with his mother, Natalie. At the age of five Peter was entrusted to a tutor who was soon impressed by the quick mind and insatiable curiosity of the boy. As co-tsar from the age of ten, Peter witnessed bloody scenes at court, involving the Old Believers, which he could neither forget nor forgive.

The Streltsy who supported Sophie were mostly Old Believers and were extreme reactionaries. Sophie, on the other hand, had western proclivities and favored educational policies advocated by a handful of progressive men who urged the study of Latin and the reading of secular books. All this finally caused the Old Believers to suspect religious perversion. It produced a tense atmosphere at the court accompanied by revolts and ugly scenes, which Peter was compelled to observe and which he always associated with the Old Believers. He must secretly have sworn to settle scores with those who had caused him and his family many hours of anguish.

The political situation of two minors sitting on a single throne created endless difficulties. Ivan was a negligible quantity, but Peter was an entirely different story. As he advanced in years he came to express definite views concerning the regency of his ambitious half-sister Sophie superimposed upon the dual rule. Peter was never able to forgive her connivings, along with the plottings and religious bigotry of the Streltsy. Gradually he came to hate all of them and cherish the hope that the hour of reckoning was bound to come.

In the spring of 1682 Sophie compelled the mother-dowager and her son Peter to move to Preobrazhenskoye, a nearby village and former summer residence of Tsar Alexis. At this place of virtual banishment Peter and his mother spent the early years of the dual reign while Sophie ruled in Moscow. Peter, however, kept busy with all sorts of schemes for his future ascendancy and handling his opponents. After his tutoring stopped, Peter began to play military games with local boys and to form his later famed regiments.

At Preobrazhenskoye Peter for the first time came across a boat that a German had built at one time for his ancestor and which, it was explained to him, had sails that could move not only with but against the wind. From that day onward Peter was interested in boats. From the local Pereyaslavl Lake to the Caspian Sea, which he saw for the first time in 1693, he continued to drive toward the sea. While at Preobrazhenskoye he summoned foreigners from the nearby "German Colony" to teach him military and naval sciences. The German colony was one of those typical European communities dwelling at that time in "Asian Muscovy." Under this first foreign influence Peter realized how far his country was behind and how much he himself had to learn. Under the tutorship of a certain German carpenter, Franz Timmermann, Peter learned about the use of an astrolabe and devoted himself to the study of mathematical sciences. From other foreign residents Peter learned about the West, which came to fascinate him.

**Peter Comes of Age.** The education which Peter received was at best casual and mostly through his own efforts. He studied mathematics avidly, was fascinated by the science of ship construction, and loved manual labor. By the time he reached seventeen years of age he had developed into a handsome giant with enormous physical strength; his social manner, however, was by no means courtly. By nature he was simple, honest, unpretentious, hard-working; he never asked for special considerations nor expected others to request them. He demanded from each as much hard work as he himself would render. He anticipated above all else loyalty and devotion not to himself but to the state, which he literally worshiped. The church he came to regard as a stagnant institution that stood in the path of progress. The Old Believers he abhorred as the enemy of the state and mercilessly chased them from pillar to post. Peter could never forget nor forgive them for their frequent revolts and was never able to erase the dark memories of his boyhood. He initiated reforms which had already been in the air for some time, but Peter was impatient and believed that their progress was too slow. He accelerated social changes to such a degree that the people came to interpret the course of events as the reign of the devil and regard the Tsar as the incarnation of Antichrist.

**Assumption of Power.** In 1689 Peter managed to rally enough support to force his sister to take the veil and disperse her favorites. Once he had assured himself of power in the capital he began a drive toward the Black Sea. In 1695 Peter opened an attack against the Turkish fortress of Azov and failed badly. This did not dishearten him and after another year of intensive preparations he renewed the onslaught and captured his goal. It was a short-lived victory, yet rewarding in the sense that it justified further efforts to transform the land-locked Russian state into a modern naval power.

**Travel Abroad.** In the capital, meanwhile, events compelled Peter to alter his plans. In 1694 Peter's mother died, followed two years later by his half-brother Ivan V. Thus freed from family problems, Peter took, in 1697, a most extraordinary step: he went abroad to visit western Europe. (*See Readings Nos. 3 and 4.*) With Peter went a large mission headed by his friend Franz Lefort, from the German Colony. Peter himself went under the assumed name of Peter Mikhailov. Since his first aim was to study naval science, it is no wonder that the countries he chose were England and Holland, where he spent most of his time. At first he settled in Holland in the little town of Saardam, where he worked in the shipyards as a carpenter. Later, when he was detected or identified, he moved to Amsterdam, where he worked in the shipyards of the East-India Company. In his free hours he studied or else visited factories, museums, schools, hospitals, and the observatory. After four months in Amsterdam he moved on to England. Just as in 1682 his early learning was interrupted by the revolt of the Streltsy, so now some fifteen years later, it was again interrupted by news of another Streltsy rebellion.

Irritable by nature, Peter now lost all patience and

hurried home to settle matters once and for all. Several hundred members of the Streltsy were executed, others were subjected to severe corporal punishment, and the military units were dissolved. From that time on Peter came to dedicate all his attention to problems at home.

**The "Rebel-Tsar."** Peter's physical appearance alone was enough to suggest the extraordinary personality of this sovereign. Extremely—almost abnormally—tall, with piercing eyes and a large face, he often suffered from a nervous tic caused, as some believe, by the ghastly scenes he witnessed in his childhood in the Kremlin palace. His figure stood out no matter where he went, for his height was almost seven feet. As he marched he swung his long arms and paced so that anyone accompanying him was almost forced to run. He possessed an unbelievable physical strength: he could break a horseshoe with his bare hands. Any man whom Peter deigned to pat on the back would suffer for some days. Peter was a bundle of contradictions: he would be unable to harm "an innocent bird" and yet with his own hand he decapitated some of the Old Believers after his return from abroad. He was liable to commit atrocities and at the same time demonstrate the kindest of sentiments one of which, incidentally, caused his death: Late in the fall of 1724, he plunged into icy water to help some sailors save their boat, and caught a severe cold, resulting in pneumonia that ended his life. Whatever he did was done to extremes. He could work for many hours without a moment's rest or plunge with a vengeance into relaxation which could turn into a bacchanalia. His humor was often crude, offensive, in poor taste, or even blasphemous. On one occasion he made twelve "cardinals" carry the "Pope" through the streets while the latter kept driving the cardinals by hitting their heads with a hammer. Later he made the "Pope" sail the Neva river in a tub filled with beer and occasionally ducked him. A heavy drinker, Peter carelessly undermined his health. At all times moody, when in low spirits he was impossible. When he felt that he had committed a wrong he was ready humbly to beg forgiveness. He hated liars and boasters: Once, when a foreign officer started to tell obviously untrue tales about valorous deeds, Peter listened for a while, soon lost patience, spat into the officer's face, and went away.

Despite the fact that Peter succeeded in establishing the Russian Empire, power never intoxicated him. He continued to lead a relatively modest private life, wearing darned socks, for example, and a worn coat. He was extremely careful with state revenues: expenses for maintenance of the court were reduced from fifteen to four per cent of the national revenues. He preferred a home-like intimacy to the cold spaciousness of the palace rooms. In France he was assigned to a room the ceiling of which was too high for his taste and he ordered an artificial ceiling made from a sail. In the new capital of St. Petersburg he built a summer and winter palace, both very small. For this reason all state entertainment was carried out in the Senate building or in the palace owned by Menshikov, or, in summer, in the open air of the garden.

And there was a marked difference in the frequency of the Tsar's public appearances and in his general manner. Formerly, a tsar would appear only on solemn occasions surrounded by dignitaries, and the public could hardly catch a glimpse of him. Peter, on the other hand, appeared alone in a Dutch sailor jacket, with a pipe between his teeth. Nothing irritated him more than courtly manners and etiquette. He was bored with official receptions, relieved when they were over; he would dash to change clothes and hurry back to the first place he could find next to some foreign merchants or a craft that interested him. He travelled throughout Russia, learned much and showed an interest in handicraft. His own hands revealed calluses which he proudly displayed in order "to demonstrate an example to others." The only thing he enjoyed during social occasions was dancing. Abstract ideas were alien to his mind, nor did he show any interest in current political philosophies. Occasionally, however, he showed an intuitive understanding of what was meant by the "common good."

**The Streltsy Rebellion.** While in Vienna Peter learned of some alarming developments taking place in Moscow. Taking advantage of his departure, Sophie returned to the capital in an attempt to recapture power. Without delay Peter abandoned his original plan of visiting Italy and hastened home to handle the situation. As soon as he returned to Moscow he forced both Sophie and his own wife to take the veil. Other participants in the plot paid more dearly, some with banishment, others with their lives. The time of the Streltsy, who supported Sophie, now ran short. When another rebellion broke out in Astrakhan in 1705, Peter decided to settle matters once and for all; the restless garrisons that muddled with their narrow religious faith were disbanded entirely.

**The Northern War.** Shortly after Peter's return the country entered the so-called Northern War with Sweden, which with the exception of a few brief intervals lasted for two decades. The basic cause of the war was the old aspiration for an outlet to the Baltic. Having attained a partial and short-lived victory in the south with the capture of Azov, Peter thought it time to renew the struggle in the north. By means of the Northern War Peter hoped to "open the window" to the West. It was a daring undertaking since it involved a struggle against a powerful European state. Sweden at the beginning of the eighteenth century was virtual master of northern Europe; since 1648 the Baltic was for all purposes a Swedish lake. And so Russia allied herself with Poland and Denmark in their common jealousy of Swedish power.

Young, impetuous Charles XII was in no mood to sit and wait until this insolent alliance became formidable. In 1700 he decided to strike hard at each of the allies separately. First came Denmark, which Charles disposed of within a week, forcing that country to sue for peace. Next he decided to concentrate on Russia. By the end of November, 1700, Swedish and Russian forces faced each other at Narva; after a brief encounter the poorly seasoned Russian army yielded ground. Charles assumed that the threat of Russia was no longer serious and he therefore turned to Poland. By making this assumption and altering the forthcoming campaign Charles committed his fatal blunder, for Swedish preoccupation in Poland allowed Peter the precious time he needed for recovery.

Charles calculated that the victory he enjoyed over Denmark would be repeated elsewhere. In Poland he planned to drive Augustus off the throne and place there a king of his own choice. Instead of moving with the lightning speed he had counted on, Charles bogged down in Poland for seven years, thereby giving Peter ample time to face Sweden in a stronger position and under more favorable circumstances. While Peter kept sending aid to Augustus II, thereby helping to prolong the war in Poland, he continued to wrest back the territory he had lost during the earlier period of the war. It was in this manner that Peter, after he captured Nöteborg (Oreshek), established a foothold on the Neva River. In May, 1703, Peter founded a fortress on one of the islets, moving the capital there from Moscow and naming it St. Petersburg.

During the following year the Russian army succeeded in occupying the Swedish provinces of Esthonia and Livonia and then moved into Courland. But Peter suddenly found himself in serious straits again when a revolt broke out in Astrakhan led for the last time by the restless Streltsy. A large portion of the army, under the able General Sheremetev, had to be diverted to quell the rebellion. The preoccupation of the Russian army in the south forced Peter to order a costly retreat. It was this temporary setback that enabled Charles XII to succeed against Augustus II, whom he dethroned and replaced with his own candidate, Stanislas Leszczynski. With both allies, Denmark and Poland, out of the war, Charles now hoped to concentrate all his attention on the Russian campaign.

For a short while it seemed as if Russia was to share the fate of her two allies. Aside from the fact that Peter was left to face his opponent entirely alone, he also encountered a critical situation at home: disturbances among the Bashkirs and the Don Cossacks diverted much of his attention, precious ammunition, and valuable manpower. Charles was so encouraged by these developments that he seriously contemplated a direct march on Moscow. By the end of September, 1708, the Swedish army found itself deep inside Russia, and the winter months were approaching fast. Instead of retreating temporarily to safer winter quarters, Charles rejected sober counsel and decided at the last minute to adopt a new strategy: instead of marching toward Moscow he turned south, hopeful of a milder winter, more adequate provisions and, above all, military assistance from Ukrainian separatists. To this end he offered an alliance to Hetman Mazeppa.

The campaign to date had already proved a serious

drain on the Swedish army, though Charles expected additional aid to reach him from Livonia. But the army sent from Livonia was intercepted and completely destroyed by the middle of October, 1708. To make things worse, Charles failed to establish direct contact with Mazeppa and Swedish efforts to cross the Desna River were effectively checked. Pressed hard, Charles now sought aid from Turkey and Poland, but neither showed any eagerness to come to his rescue. It was amid these frustrated efforts that the Swedish army reached the southernmost point in the Ukraine, Poltava, where the historic battle took place on July 8, 1709. The outcome was virtually predetermined. The Swedes, though all seasoned soldiers, were outnumbered; they lacked ammunition; they were too far from their home base, and exhausted from continuous campaigning. The Russians, on the other hand, had everything their opponents lacked. The Swedish army put up a stubborn resistance, but it fought against too many odds and in the end had to surrender to the superior Russian forces. Charles narrowly escaped capture and together with Mazeppa made his way into Turkey.

**The Poltava Victory.** The battle of Poltava marked the end of Sweden's meteoric rise to power. On the other hand, it was an opening chapter in Russian history and a great personal triumph for Peter I. The defeat of Sweden, however, came dear: the economic strain caused by the continuous struggle left the country in a state of almost complete exhaustion. What was worse, despite the defeat of the enemy the war continued, lasting for no less than twelve more years. Meanwhile, taking advantage of the brief respite, Peter revenged himself on the Cossacks for betraying him: thenceforth their autonomy gradually diminished and the office of the Hetman became a mere shadow. Furthermore, the defeat of Sweden marked the beginning of Poland's decline. It was only to be expected that the Russian triumph also caused the removal of Leszczynski from the Polish throne and the reinstatement, with Peter's aid, of Augustus II.

By the end of 1710 the entire coast of the Baltic was under Russian control and this in turn indirectly aided the expulsion of Sweden from Pomerania. By 1713 Peter had managed to deliver the Swedish navy serious blows

with his recently constructed flotilla, which seized Helsing-
fors, Åbo, and later the important base of Hangö, including the strategic Aaland Islands. By the end of 1714
virtually all of Finland was in Russian hands. In order to
establish Russian sovereignty or future claim thereon
Peter adopted the strategy of the Habsburgs—royal
matrimony. His half-niece Anna, daughter of Ivan V,
Peter married to the Polish vassal, the Duke of Courland.
A second half-niece, Catherine, Peter married in 1716 to
the Duke of Mecklenburg. A year later, while visiting
Versailles, Peter hoped to arrange another marriage, that
of his daughter Elizabeth to Louis XV, but this plan
never materialized. The ascendancy of Russia in the
northwest, replacing Sweden, was a factor of incalculable
historical importance.

    **The Aftermath.** Encouraged by recent victories,
Peter revived the often tried scheme against the Ottoman
Empire, but here he dismally failed. An expedition dispatched to Azov suffered total defeat and Peter dourly
consented to sign the peace in 1711. By the Treaty of
Prut Turkey regained Azov while Russia was obligated
to demolish her recently constructed fortifications. It was
left to Catherine II to accomplish what Peter I had so
vainly tried more than a half a century before.

    The Northern War dragged on and the impression at
times was given that Sweden would never yield until she
regained her former power. When, however, in 1719 and
again a year later, Russian troops successfully landed on
the coast of Sweden the final verdict had to be accepted.
France offered mediation and Sweden consented to terminate the protracted conflict in 1721. According to the
Treaty of Nystadt Sweden relinquished to Russia Livonia,
Esthonia, Ingria, Carelia, a small part of Finland in the
southeast, and the valuable islands of Oesel and Dago
that guarded the entrance to the Finnish Gulf. For the
Peace of Nystadt, the culmination of his triumph, Peter
was rewarded by his grateful government with the title
of "Emperor" and the epithet "the Great."

    **Imperial Russia.** Henceforth Russia was established
as a great power on the Baltic coast. If Peter could sadly
observe the loss of Azov and the more recent acquisitions
along the Caspian Sea in the south, in the north he was
able to rejoice over his triumph, the establishment of

Russian sovereignty on the banks of the Neva and on the shores of the Baltic. From his new capital of St. Petersburg Peter could gaze through the misty air over the Gulf of Finland and contemplate his beloved country as the future maritime power in Europe.

**Domestic Affairs.** In domestic affairs Peter's goals varied. One of his aims was to wrench the state from sloth to efficiency. Another was to use wasted manpower. This called for streamlining the civil service, with a re-definition of loyalty, and an alteration of the social structure. A prolonged peace was necessary to the accomplishment of Peter's goals, yet foreign aims continuously kept the country in a state of war.

**"The Table of Ranks."** Peter's intention was to see that every subject contributed service to the state. Because of Russia's chronic warring during Peter's reign military service became the most widely exacted form of service. Second only to the demands of war were those of the economy. Peter's plans involved construction of the new capital, of canals, harbors, and other improvements, for which purpose legions of men had been commandeered by daily decrees. The nobility regardless of seniority, rank, or eminence was also expected to serve the state. Shirkers were penalized; diligence was richly rewarded. As an incentive Peter set up the "Table of Ranks," which established a nobility of service to replace the nobility of birth. Henceforth all had to begin serving from the lowest rank and climb according to merit only. The hereditary nobility had every reason to criticize the new decree, but was incapable of doing anything else as long as Peter ruled the country.

This mandatory service to the state resulted in a social levelling best demonstrated by the Regiments of the Guard, which became the base at which young noblemen from all over Russia gathered to start their social careers. During the reign of Peter the regiments were a tool in the mighty hands of the sovereign. However, in time of weaker successors throughout the decades immediately following Peter I, the same regiments reversed the process, seating and unseating sovereigns at their pleasure.

**Other Reforms.** Peter's great designs required enormous financial and economic resources. Tax assessments

were increased, and men throughout the country ex-
plored the potential wealth of national resources. The old
form of taxing households was found entirely inadequate
and therefore was replaced by a capitation tax, which
soon fell short of all expectations. The problem was
solved simply by adding to the inadequate results of the
capitation tax various other forms of exactions. By the
end of Peter's reign there was hardly an article in the
land that had escaped being taxed.

Ministerial Colleges. From the start Peter realized
that the old administrative system badly needed an over-
haul. The Boyar Council and the *Prikazy,* or Departments, proved cumbersome and inefficient. After a brief
survey abroad Peter chose the Swedish administrative
system as the most suitable. The Boyar Council was replaced by a body with the high-sounding name of Senate,
and the antiquated Departments were replaced by Ministerial Colleges. At the beginning, the chief duty of the
Senate, which was appointed by the Crown, was to serve
temporarily while the Tsar was absent from the capital,
as frequently happened in the case of Peter I. Eventually
the Senate was assigned a multitude of duties of executive
and judicial nature to be supervised as a "Procurator-
General." Local government was streamlined by having
the country divided into provinces, or *gubernias.* The
towns were given the right to set up their municipal governments. The church, too, underwent a drastic administrative change. The office of Patriarch was abolished and
replaced by the Holy Synod, which subjected the church
to state control as never before. The head of the newly
organized Synod was also called Procurator-General. The
post was held by a layman appointed by the Crown.

Whatever reforms Peter introduced fit a common pattern—a utilitarian application of his generally conceived
national plans. Thus, when Peter spoke of enlightenment
and ordered books from abroad he had in mind the applied sciences serving economic and military ends; when
he ordered young men to study abroad he expected them
to return better equipped with technical skill and information to be utilized by the state. Even in the case of
the Russian alphabet Peter thought as he looked at it of
how it could be altered and made more practical. Exam-
ining the old ornamental and antiquated letters he con-

cluded that it did not suit modern needs. In his characteristic arbitrary manner, which must have shocked orthodox
linguists, he simplified the alphabet, introduced numerous
foreign terms, and made the Russian language what it is
today.

**The Impact upon Russia.** Politically, Russia under
Peter I became a more solidified monarchy. The Boyar
Council, declining during the seventeenth century, was
effectively finished by 1700. Under Peter's guidance the
crown succeeded in concentrating more power than ever
before. The social structure was streamlined by giving
official recognition to only three classes—the nobility, the
bourgeoisie, and the peasantry, the last consisting either
of freemen or serfs. The only tie that held all classes
together was the direct or indirect service all were to
render to the state. In his effort to compel everyone to
serve the state, Peter used all possible means of compulsion. He delegated authority to the landlord over the
serf; simultaneously he saw to it that the state exercised
virtually unrestrained power over the nobility. Furthermore, he established primogeniture, thereby forcing the
younger sons of the nobility to go into service. For the
same reason he forbade any man under thirty to join
monastic orders. All this was in effect during Peter's
lifetime. Shortly after his death the aristocracy, displeased
with its status as defined by Peter, managed to shake off
many of its former obligations to the state. It succeeded,
however, in retaining the obligatory services imposed
upon other classes, mainly upon the peasantry. In this
manner it brought upon itself and the country complex
problems that altered the course of Russian history for
more than a century.

**The Petrine Era and After.** Peter's entire life was
dedicated to the state and he never had time to devote
attention either to himself or to his family. Yet seldom
had the fate of the state been linked so closely to the
royal family and the succession as in the case of Peter I.
Personal negligence on the part of Peter led to family
complications which in turn were bound to bear grave
political consequences. To begin with, Peter married the
daughter of a prominent family, Evdokiya Lopukhina,
at the age of seventeen. A greater conflict in personalities
could hardly be imagined. His wife proved to be deeply

conservative and detested everything dear to her husband. Out of this marriage came one son, Alexis, who spent most of his youth with his mother while his father wandered throughout the country, dashing from one battlefront to another, or travelling abroad. The inevitable result was that his mother succeeded in alienating the boy from his father. When in 1696 Peter discovered that his wife was implicated in plotting while he was abroad, he banished her to a monastery and entrusted his sister with the care of Alexis. It was not too long before he discovered that this arrangement was equally unsatisfactory.

The Case of Alexis. At the age of twenty-one Alexis was sent abroad by his father. The latter hoped that his son's education might be profitable. Alexis set out for western Europe with great reluctance: by prearrangement he was married to Princess Charlotte of the House of Brunswick. Charlotte died in 1715 and left two children, a daughter Natalia, and a son named Peter. Meanwhile, the father impatiently began to press his "useless son" Alexis to assume greater responsibility in state affairs. Alexis in turn asked if he might resign, but Peter would not listen to such nonsense and threatened to send him to a monastery. What Peter feared most, and for good reason, was that eventually Alexis might become the center of a plot to return the court to its "Muscovite days."

When Peter was abroad again in November, 1717, Alexis packed up his personal belongings and, together with a concubine, fled to Austria, where he sought the protection of Charles VI. (Eventually Alexis moved south and settled near Naples.) When Peter heard the news he could not rest until the culprit was brought back. He employed every means to track him and persuade the single heir to the throne to return home. Alexis finally consented to do so provided he would be permitted to renounce the throne, return to the countryside, and marry the girl with whom he had escaped. Upon his return Alexis renounced the throne and was pardoned. Yet further investigations of the case revealed that Alexis was involved in a far more serious plot than had been realized, involving the murder of his father with foreign aid. A special commission appointed by Peter scrutinized the evidence and recommended a death sentence. In November, 1718, the sentence was carried out, leaving Alexis' son Peter as the only direct descendant and legitimate heir to the throne. The question of succession became more involved than ever.

**Who Next?** After Peter divorced his first wife in 1712 he married a girl he had met some years earlier during the war with Sweden. From this marriage came twelve children—four sons and eight daughters, of whom only two daughters, Anna and Elizabeth, survived. In February, 1721, on the spur of the moment, Peter decreed that the sovereign had the right to name his own successor, though he failed to do so in his own case. In December, 1724, while saving some drowning sailors in the Neva, Peter contracted a severe cold. He disregarded his condition and early in January attended an outdoor religious ceremony. He soon became gravely ill and suddenly died while endeavoring to dictate his will. This left the question of succession in complete confusion, and for the next four decades or so it was determined capriciously by the Regiments of the Guard.

— 5 —

# THE PERIOD OF COURT REVOLUTIONS, 1725-62

**The Reign of Catherine I.** Between 1725 and 1762 the Regiments of the Guard determined the fate of the throne and the choice of the sovereign. Personalities like Peter I do not appear frequently in the pages of history. The handful of his admirers who aspired to power and influence after his death were dwarfs by his side. They lacked the vision, the audacity, the driving force, and the conviction of the giant removed from the scene of political life. They were incapable of comprehending the broad implications of the Petrine era or of projecting themselves into the future and realizing its historic importance for the generations to follow. What interested these men most was how they could cast off their burdens of obligatory service by shifting them onto others. For the following three quarters of the century a two-pronged development may be observed: on one hand, the expansion and entrenchment of serfdom; on the other, the emancipation and consolidation of the serf-owning gentry. By 1762 the nobility had managed to secure complete freedom; by 1785 it won a Charter which specifically formulated its privileged position in society.

A glance at the occupants of the throne and their fate from the death of Peter I, in 1725, to the rise of Catherine II, in 1762, is most illuminating. In accordance with past experience in the absence of a male heir, the throne would have to pass to Elizabeth and not the wife of the deceased sovereign. (See the genealogical table.) However, those who came to power decided differently. Some of them favored Peter's widow, Catherine, while others preferred Peter II, son of the executed Alexis. No one seemed to have given any thought at all to Elizabeth. Since the army overwhelmingly supported Catherine and they in turn were supported by Peter I's immediate aides —Count Tolstoy, Baron (later Count) Ostermann, Prince Menshikov, Admiral Apraksin, and Procurator-General of the Senate Yaguzhinski—the choice was predetermined: Catherine I was proclaimed Empress of Russia. In a sense it marked a victory for the followers of Peter I against the old aristocracy: it rendered impossible any restoration of the Muscovites.

**The Brief Reign of Peter II.** Catherine's rule was short-lived and the end of her reign was foreseen weeks before her death. For this reason the Guards took up the matter of succession during her last few months, realizing that the candidacy of Peter's grandson could no longer be disregarded. Of the possible candidates, Peter ranked first on the list, followed by two of Peter I's daughters, and a granddaughter, Natalia. The twelve-year-old boy, son of Alexis and grandson of Peter I, was duly proclaimed successor to the vacant throne. The election of Peter signified a victory of a different kind: in a political sense it carried anti-Petrine forebodings, an effort to turn the wheel of history backward which was best expressed in the decision to transfer the court back to the old capital in Moscow. This scheme was sponsored by two eminent families, the Golitsyns and the Dolgorukis. The latter were prominent at court, exerted great influence upon Peter II, and, incidentally, hoped to have the new sovereign marry the daughter of Alexis Dolgoruki. On the other hand, Menshikov, who wielded considerable power at court before the ascendancy of Peter II, was now banished from the capital. But the victory of the diehards, the Muscovite part, proved of short duration: at a hunting party the young emperor caught a cold and died on the very day that had been set for his marriage to Princess Dolgoruki. Not only did this upset the Dolgoruki calculations, but it also marked the end of the male line of Romanovs. Who had the right to the throne and who had the power to solve the dynastic riddle at this turn of events, were the two most bewildering issues at the death of Peter II. In desperation Dolgoruki tried to seat Peter's betrothed on the vacated throne. He even forged a will to that effect, but it proved a complete failure.

Plans for a "Russian Magna Charta." For the historical record the new occurrence deserves mention. Taking advantage of the situation after Peter II's death, a group of nobles made an effort to limit the absolute power of the crown by having the candidate sign a list of "Conditions." One of the effects of Peter I's reforms was that western political institutions had come under Russian purview and some of the nobility had acquainted themselves with the means whereby absolutism might be restrained by the aristocracy. To this end several of the aristocratic families, in coöperation with the higher ranks of the bureaucracy, formed in 1726 a so-called Supreme Council made up of six, and later of eight, members. The original purpose was to bring into harmony the conflicting views of the old and recently formed aristocratic elements. This Council assumed the role of an upper chamber with power to curb the monarch. The Council's feigned authority had already been questioned at the time of Peter II, though ineffectively. When in 1730 Peter II suddenly died, the Council took advantage of the temporary confusion to assert its authority. Directly following the death announcement, the Council members gathered hastily and hoped by co-opting additional members of the families of Golitsyn and Dolgoruki, to strengthen their cause before undertaking a discussion of the forthcoming succession.

The main figure among the eight Councilmen was undoubtedly Prince D. M. Golitsyn. He was one of the most enlightened men of his time in Russia, a firm westerner who believed in reforms which, he hastened to qualify, should advance slowly in order to avoid a sudden break with national traditions. Golitsyn's arguments were that the male line of the imperial dynasty had ended, and that there were no legitimate heirs after Peter I's death. Catherine I's testament must be disregarded, for as a woman of lower social origin, she had no real right to the throne and therefore could not legitimately will it to anyone else; likewise, the will of Peter II, presumably passing the crown to his fiancée, Princess Dolgoruki, must be brushed aside as a forgery. Having disposed thus of the possible candidacy of Elizabeth as the illegitimate daughter of Peter I at the time of her birth, the Council resolved that Anne, the half-niece of Peter I and presently widowed Duchess of Courland, might be regarded as the only lawful claimant. To her should be offered the crown provided she consented to recognize the status of the Council and accepted certain "Conditions."

**Candidacy of Anne.** Next day the Council appeared before the joint assembly of the Senate, the Synod, and other political and military leaders, to announce their choice—without, however, mentioning the intended "Conditions." After the Council obtained the approval of Anne's candidacy the members gathered to draw up their "Magna Charta." The document stipulated that Anne, upon accepting the crown, must pledge neither to marry nor to name a successor, declare neither war nor peace, impose no taxes nor disburse public funds, make no land grants, confiscate no property, nor impose death penalties, unless the Council grant its unanimous consent. Violation of this pledge would be equivalent to renunciation of the throne. Anne signed the document and returned it to Moscow. (*See Reading No. 5.*)

Several members voiced their misgivings. They argued

that there were influential relations and admirers of Anne who were against the curbing of absolutism, and that these persons anticipated making their own gains as long as Anne had no legal restraints. Among the latter were the Saltykovs, Romodanovs, and Golovkins, later to be joined by members of the "German party." There were also others who were skeptical about the document—noblemen who were jealous of the possible gains the others represented in the Council might make if the enterprise proved successful. Among the latter were representatives of such families as the Trubetskois, Yaguzhinskis, and Kantemirs, and the high clergy headed by the well-known leader Feofan Prokopovich. The Guards Regiments also looked askance at the "Conditions," and argued that their adoption would result in "ten autocratic families instead of one absolute sovereign." The military elements were against any oligarchic regime and predicted that a limited monarchy would prove a dangerous political system to the country especially in time of war. It was clear that the neglected "Estates-General," as the well-known contemporary historian Tatishchev envisioned correctly, if not summoned to participate in government would prefer the retention of absolutism.

**A Constitutional Fiasco.** While these negotiations were going on behind the scenes, important developments had taken place in Moscow. Representatives of the high and lesser nobility, the high officials, members of the Regiments of the Guards, and others who had assembled in that city for the royal wedding found themselves attending a royal funeral. They then witnessed not only the election of a new sovereign but discovered that the Council had secretly schemed to impose royal limitations. The prevailing sentiment among the assembled representatives was that the Council had acted autocratically. Some objected violently to such self-asserted rights, others opposed the very existence of the Council, while still others did not mind its functioning provided its membership would include a wider representative group of the nobility.

The decisive moment was reached on February 13 when the reply was delivered from Anne which confirmed the "Conditions." The Council then appeared before the assembly to reveal for the first time the precise nature of the document, which thus far had been kept entirely secret. The affair was mainly engineered by Prince Golitsyn and it proved as risky a game as it was unscrupulously played. To Anne he stated that the "Conditions" expressed the general will of the entire nobility; to the gathered assembly in Moscow he explained that the terms represented a voluntary act obtained without coercion, conceived and granted at the initiative of Anne. If among the ranks of the aristocracy there was no agreement as to how autocracy might be curbed, the members of the Guards unanimously agreed that there should be no tampering with the authority of the sovereign. Rather than take orders from eight inflexible councilmen the Guards preferred to have a female sovereign who would be given unlimited power—as long, of course, as she was pliant enough to serve their wishes. The debate grew agitated; the Council faced strong opposition. Their opponents offered all kinds of solutions, none of which, however, would include in any form the plan proposed by the Council.

**Anne Retains Absolute Power.** Amidst these discussions and conflicts Anne made her entrance into Moscow on February 26. She quickly sensed the political tension and felt reasonably certain that the Guards would stand by her side. On the very day of her arrival the high officials assembled to take a loyalty oath to the new Empress which contained no reference to the "Conditions." After that Anne was presented with two petitions, one of which requested administrative reforms, the other of which pleaded that she retain absolute power. Her reply was curt: she declared that her signature to the "Conditions" was obtained fraudulently, since she was given the impression that this was the unanimous decision. Then she publicly tore up the signed document. There was nothing left but to take the oath to Anne, Autocrat and Empress of All the Russias. The Guards could celebrate a political victory over their court opponents: the premature plot to inaugurate a Russian Magna Charta was successfully foiled. It is doubtful whether the general public even knew that the country had come within inches of getting its first constitution.

**Personality of Anne.** The predictions of men like Golitsyn proved prophetic. Anne assumed absolute rule amidst conflicting views and interests which enabled her to use one contending side against the other while strengthening her own position, and at the same time obligated herself neither to individuals nor to any group. All available accounts concerning the personality of Anne do not have much to say in her favor. Officially Anne was the daughter of Ivan V. Yet her paternity has been gravely doubted, Ivan being physically an extremely feeble man. The first thing that impressed people about the Empress was her huge awkward figure, her coarse masculine voice, and her rough manners, acquired in self-defense against her domineering mother.

Peter I arranged Anne's marriage at the age of fifteen to the Duke of Courland. Since the Duchy was a fief of Poland the marriage carried with it obvious political motivation—to weaken Polish prestige. But her husband died within twelve months of their marriage, and there followed years of lonely, dull widowhood in the alien atmosphere of Mitau. Her life was haunted by the suspicion that her Russian relatives had abandoned her; she feared constantly that the Poles might rob her of her tiny realm. Anne might have felt abandoned, yet the court at St. Petersburg continued to interfere with her private life, and to restrain her political freedom and even personal plans, for she was forbidden to remarry.

Possessed of an avid thirst for luxurious living, Anne was forced to subsist on a niggardly allowance. The embarrassment caused by this condition, and her natural ill temper, resulted in her carrying a deep grudge against everyone for her unhappy lot. The fact that she was not blessed with any physical attraction did not help her humor. Such was the woman who suddenly, by a stroke of good fortune, found herself on the throne of the Russian Empire. At first she had to face the humiliation of acceding to the "Conditions" that limited her power and extracted from her the promise not to marry without the approval of the Council, although in the end the "Conditions" were cast aside and she assumed the crown of an absolute monarch. At the time Anne reached the throne she was in her middle thirties, at an age when her character was completely crystallized and her habits, tastes, manners, and views well set. She demonstrated an absence of feminine tenderness; she engaged in masculine sports, and was fond of hunting, horsemanship, and sharpshooting. Anne used to keep a loaded rifle in the palace to shoot birds that would pass by the window. In March, 1737, she boasted of shooting a wild boar with her own hands. Her favorite game was rabbits, ducks, wild goats, and deer.

Anne loved a long siesta after her noon meal, then would listen to a girls' chorus performing folksongs, watch a court jester, or have one of the maids narrate some folk tales. Her harsh character may be explained by a subconscious ambition to revenge herself for what she thought were insults and injuries committed by her kin prior to her ascendancy to power. Anne often referred to her relatives as "ungrateful slaves" and derived pleasure in seeing them cower around the throne. She enjoyed ordering some of the court dignitaries to play the role of clown; on one occasion she even forced M. A. Golitsyn to divorce his wife and then marry an ugly native woman of Kamchatka. Though indifferent to religion she feigned once in a while to be zealously faithful to the Orthodox Church. Once she slapped the face of a princess who had embraced the Roman Catholic faith.

During her reign legal punishment such as tongue clipping, public whipping, or mutilation of nostrils, was considered an act of royal compassion. Torture of those sentenced to death was a common practice. Even Anne's wit often expressed itself in crude forms. Arrogant, wavering, Anne at the same time was rather secretive and her facial expression would never betray either emotional sensitivity or a kindly thought. Some of her courtiers explained her inconstancy by her complete submission to the will of her Chancellor, Biron, regardless of what her personal feelings might be. Anne was suspicious and trusted very few. The handful of courtiers who did enjoy her confidence were mostly Baltic Germans who came with her from Courland.

**The Reign of Anne, 1730-40.** It was almost with a vengeance that Anne plunged into the life of extravagance only recently forbidden to her in Mitau. Nor did her lack of refinement help improve the atmosphere at the court of St. Petersburg. Coarse in manners, crude in tastes, she brought to court an air of vulgarity that shocked many. Prince Golitsyn, who championed without success the adoption of the "Conditions," could at least find dubious vindication in the fact that Anne came to demonstrate his contention that irresponsible absolutism must breed purposeless tyranny. Being a vindictive woman she was never able to forgive the former members of the Council for daring to limit her power. Shortly after her ascendancy she took joy in pillorying them, banishing them to Siberia, stripping them of their property. During her ten-year reign the Secret Chancellory ruled supreme, while the Baltic favorites who accompanied her assumed unrestrained authority in high offices. Among these may be mentioned the notorious Biron, the Loewenwold brothers, Ostermann, for seventeen years head of the Foreign Office, and Münnich, Commander-in-Chief of the Russian Army.

Shortly after the coronation of Anne the court returned to the northern capital of St. Petersburg. Ostensibly Anne followed the policy of westernization set out by Peter I. But whereas court life under Peter I was never noted for extravagance, under Anne ostentatious living became a serious drain upon the economy. Whereas the tax burden under Peter I was heavy, at least it was justifiable, being honestly disbursed for national development. Under Anne, however, the increased burdens were hardly comprehensible since few could claim benefits therefrom. Aside from court expenditures the maintenance of the Guards had also risen, since two more regiments were added to the two original ones. To aggravate matters further, most of the officers of the newly formed Guards units were of German extraction. If Anne ever succeeded in forging unity among the ranks of the nobility, including the Guards, it was by swelling the ranks of high appointees with Germans. The opportunity for demonstration of discontent came in the fall of 1740 when Anne died, and once more the country had to decide the question of succession.

**Problem of Succession.** Since Anne was a childless widow she named as her successor Ivan, a half-great-great nephew of Peter I. The devious genealogical line in this case calls for an explanatory note. The sister of Empress Anne, Catherine, was married to Charles Leopold, Duke of Mecklenburg. In 1718 a daughter was born to them named Anna, better known as Anna Leopoldovna. In

1740 the latter married Prince Antony Ulrich of Bruns-wick-Bevern. It was their offspring, Ivan, born during the same year, that Anne named as her successor. This two-month-old infant, known as Ivan VI, reigned exactly thirteen months. Because Ivan's parents had some serious family difficulties and were living apart, Anne, shortly before her death, named Biron as regent.

The news of Biron's appointment was most disturbing to the Guards, who were ready to take action at once. Indignation rose particularly when a rumor spread that Biron intended to remove the Guards from any possible political influence in the future. The position of Biron was further challenged by his strong contestant, Field Marshal Münnich, who presumably stood for the rights of the successor's parents against the ambitions of the regent. Hardly three weeks had passed since Anne's death when Münnich, supported by the Preobrazhensky regiment of the Guards, seized Biron during the night and shortly after banished him to Siberia. Having rid themselves of Biron, they proclaimed as regent the mother of Ivan VI, Anna Leopoldovna. But this woman was such a com-plete nonentity that intrigues and plots became a matter of daily routine. It was not long before Münnich's turn came: he was removed by Ostermann, who was backed for regent by Prince Antony, the father of the infant.

**The Candidacy of Elizabeth.** It was in the midst of these developments that Elizabeth, the younger daughter of Peter I by his second wife, made her entry. Born in 1709, she remained an unmarried resident of St. Peters-burg. Her popularity among the Guards led to the in-evitable formation of a group that supported her can-didacy to the throne. They argued that as descendant of an illustrious father and a true Russian woman, Elizabeth would be able to free the government from foreign in-fluence. Ostermann immediately took action. Under the pretext that war with Sweden seemed inevitable he or-dered the removal from the capital of all troops that might support Elizabeth's candidacy. Elizabeth, her prin-cipal advisor Bestuzhev, and her favorites determined to forestall this occurrence at any cost. On December 6, 1741, Elizabeth and a group of supporters appeared at the barracks of the Preobrazhensky regiment, where the Guardsmen pledged their absolute loyalty to her. Elizabeth and her loyal supporters then marched to the palace, where they seized Ivan VI, his parents, and soon afterwards Münnich, Ostermann, and other influential courtiers. After all were safely removed and placed under arrest Elizabeth was proclaimed Empress of Russia. It marked the triumph of the "Russian" as against the "Teutonic" part of the nobility.

The plot had disastrous effects upon the Brunswick members. At first Elizabeth contemplated allowing their departure for abroad. But it was soon discovered that Elizabeth's ascendancy was not by any means met with universal approval, and events took a tragic turn. It should be noted that during the preceding reign the influence of the Guards upon political life in the capital had increased as never before. Shortly after Elizabeth assumed power, the Preobrazhensky and Izmailovsky regiments were discovered in a plot to restore Ivan VI to the throne. The unsuccessful plot of 1742 was followed a year later by another of even more serious scope, involving several high dignitaries and leading women of the court. Implicated in this Brunswick plot was the Austrian Ambassador, who wrongly regarded Elizabeth as pro-French. For this reason he favored the Brunswick branch, related to the Habsburgs, over Elizabeth.

The plotters endeavored to stir up discontent by protesting the extravagant court life and Elizabeth's lavishness. Being the illegitimate daughter of Peter I (they refused, as did the Council in 1730, to recognize Peter's second marriage), Elizabeth, they contended, had no right whatever to the throne. But the plot never materialized except in nearly causing severance of diplomatic relations with Austria. To appease the fury of the Russian Empress, Maria Theresa agreed to recall her ambassador. The plotters at home shared a worse fate. Two of the women, Mme. Bestuzheva and the famous beauty and social rival of Elizabeth, Mme. Lopukhina, were publicly whipped, their tongues were clipped, and both were banished. A third participant, Mme. Sophie Lilienfeldt, was spared similar punishment because of her pregnancy at the time. As for the Brunswick members, Elizabeth ordered their immediate return to the capital. The party had just reached Riga when the entire retinue was taken back to St. Petersburg. Ivan VI was imprisoned in the

Schlüsselburg fortress while his parents were banished north to Kholmogory.

Ivan VI lingered in his confinement until 1764, when he perished under rather mysterious circumstances. His mother, not able to endure the hardships of exile, passed away in 1746; Ivan's father, Prince Antony, lived until 1775. Their other children grew up without parental care or education until Catherine II ordered, in 1780, that they be given permission to leave Russia. Reluctantly they accepted the verdict and were taken to Denmark where their aunt, the Danish Queen, took charge of them. The reign of Elizabeth thus terminated further infiltration of the Brunswicks and Holsteins into the Russian royal line and reduced Germanic influence at court. Biron was eventually given permission to reside in Yaroslavl; Ostermann and Field Marshal Münnich were banished to Siberia; the Dolgorukis and Golitsyns, who in recent years had been persecuted, were allowed to return to St. Petersburg and were restored to their former eminence and position.

**Reign of Elizabeth, 1741-62.** The seventy-five-year period following the death of Peter I is noted mainly for court revolutions accompanied by imprisonments, assassinations, personal extravange, and administrative corruption. Yet, following the Petrine era, the reign of Elizabeth was the first of long term, lasting two decades that are noted for both longevity and relative prosperity. For some fifteen years the country enjoyed peace, while during the rest of the reign the country conducted a successful war against Sweden. Elizabeth was also fortunate in being assisted by a number of men who, though not always scrupulous, at least manifested remarkable administrative ability and superior leadership. Among these must first be mentioned Prince P. I. Shuvalov, who was largely responsible for the wise financial policy of the country with its beneficial effect upon the general national economy.

**Personality of Elizabeth.** As the daughter of a Baltic peasant girl Elizabeth must have inherited from her mother bursting health and a cheerful disposition. Her education was elementary to say the least; she was surprised to learn, for instance, that England could not be reached by land. Though she lacked refinement Elizabeth

would occasionally demonstrate better taste than Anne.
Her very appearance conveyed greater dignity and social
grace. Her most winning quality was her natural wit. The
theater fascinated her while the ballet virtually intoxicated her. Elizabeth's greatest weakness was clothes: her
wardrobe exceeded the dreams of any royal female, running to several thousands of dresses. (*See Reading
No. 6.*)

The art of statecraft remained largely a mystery to her
throughout her lifetime. At times she demonstrated a
keen interest in promoting national welfare, yet all her
life she remained an extremely frivolous woman. Elizabeth loved or hated people largely because of personal
sentiments rather than rational motivation. She detested
and fought Prussia to the end of her days. She pledged
loyal support to Maria Theresa against Frederick II, even
—as Elizabeth declared to the Austrian Ambassador—at
the cost of selling half of her jewelry and wardrobe
should the conflict call for such sacrifice. She regarded
"Old Fritz" as nothing but a godless Voltairian, loathed
him more for his atheism than for his political ambitions,
and wondered why the Lord would not perform one of
His miracles to rid the earth of that evil king. As a
devout Orthodox Elizabeth fasted, regularly attended
church services, and hated the Old Believers, whom she
persecuted without mercy. Shortly after her ascendancy
she expressed her wish to have all Jews expelled from
Russia and to see to it that they never returned again.
While expelling them, Elizabeth believed, the authorities
must see that they did not take any money with them;
they were the enemies of Christ and as such had no
place in a Christian state.

During Anne's reign Elizabeth had led a lonely life of
her own surrounded by only a few close friends. She
grew virtually alone, so that by the time she reached the
throne her personality was formulated and her ideas,
whatever they might have been, were deeply ingrained.
State affairs bored her and she seldom attended sessions
of the Senate; she procrastinated at many of her duties;
she delayed for weeks granting audiences to persons she
did not care for; she let important papers clutter her
desk for months awaiting her signature. Statesmen often
had to employ her favorites to get her to attend to urgent

matters. On one occasion she signed a reply to a letter of Louis XV, informing her of the birth of a son, precisely three years after the receipt of the message. In 1746, it has been said, while Elizabeth was signing the treaty with Austria, a wasp landed on her quill. Barely having time to draw the first three letters of her name, she threw the quill and did not complete the signature until six weeks later. Never before was social life gayer at the court of St. Petersburg, with balls, parties, dances, and lavish entertainment.

State affairs were handled by people Elizabeth could trust. To eliminate possible abuses and to be assured that various views were adequately presented, Elizabeth had the curious policy of assigning important tasks to men professing different—at times totally contradictory— views. Thus, in the field of foreign affairs Elizabeth would assign various problems simultaneously to Chancellor A. P. Bestuzhev and Vice Chancellor M. L. Vorontsov. The former favored coöperation with England; the latter sought an alliance with France, who at that time was at war with England. Both men hated each other and each schemed to oust the other from office. Elizabeth kept vacillating between the two, and procrastinating, until events took their own course.

In these circumstances it is a marvel how much divine luck was with the Empress. In the realm of internal affairs such accomplishments might be mentioned as legislation removing restrictions upon trade and the elimination of local duties imposed upon commodities within the country. A special Commission was summoned to work on a new code of laws; the University of Moscow was founded; the Academy of Arts opened; army recruiting was considerably improved. In foreign affairs, the success of Elizabeth was due more to chance than to carefully planned strategy. Seldom had a country been so poorly prepared for war, yet the campaigns during the Seven Years' War were conducted with surprising success. The troops were inadequately equipped; the military leaders were haphazardly chosen and often proved to be notoriously incapable. Still the army managed to win battles and even invade East Prussia, seizing Königsberg and Berlin itself. Elizabeth never interfered with the conduct of the war, letting the military use their initiative and plan their own campaigns. Left to itself the army, despite all handicaps, revealed an unusual fighting quality and potential force. Of further assistance was the fact that Elizabeth did not have to carry out reforms and conduct war simultaneously, as did her father and later Catherine II.

**Effects of Elizabeth's Accession.** The immediate effect of Elizabeth's assession was a decline in German domination of the national government. The new Empress prided herself on being the daughter of an illustrious father, while her admirers regarded her as the true heiress of the Petrine legacy and the only legitimate claimant to the throne. Elizabeth was extremely patriotic though never chauvinistic. She adored Moscow yet retained the capital in St. Petersburg. She had a pronounced dislike of Germans though she was never a victim of xenophobia. She admired the French mainly because of the legendary life at Versailles rather than for cultural reasons. It was for this if for no other reason that Russian-French relations during the reign of Elizabeth became well established and French cultural influence appeared more pronounced.

**Peter III Named Elizabeth's Successor.** Shortly after ascending the throne Elizabeth named her nephew the Duke of Holstein, as her successor and requested that he transfer his residence from Kiel to Russia. In a strict sense this was a correct move since it placed on the throne the only surviving descendant of Peter I. As the son of Elizabeth's elder sister the boy had every right to claim the imperial crown of Russia. The premature concern was very likely justified in order to forestall possible conflict in the future. Thus far, Elizabeth's action was honorable and well-intended. Yet in the end, as will be subsequently noted, the wisdom of the choice might be seriously questioned.

In February, 1742, Charles Peter Ulrich, Duke of Holstein, was summoned by Elizabeth to the Russian capital. The young lad chosen to succeed Elizabeth was the only grandson of Peter I by his second marriage. In June, 1725, the elder sister of Elizabeth, Anna, in accordance with the wish of her father, Peter I, had married the Duke of Holstein-Gottorp, Charles Frederick, a nephew of Charles XII of Sweden. Shortly after the birth of their son, both parents died and the orphaned boy was regarded as heir to the throne of Sweden. For this reason he was taught Swedish and brought up in the Lutheran faith. Then suddenly, at the request of Elizabeth, Charles Peter Ulrich was wrenched from his home at Kiel, taken to Russia, given the title of Grand Duke, compelled to embrace the Orthodox faith and learn Russian, renamed Pyotr Feodorovich, later better known as Peter III, and officially proclaimed heir to the imperial throne of Russia.

**Personality of Peter III.** The Grand Duke bitterly resented the entire affair and for nearly two decades wished sullenly to revenge himself for this arbitrary decision of Elizabeth. The latter sensed his feelings but hoped that in due course Peter would become acclimated; nothing of the kind ever happened. Though brought to Russia when he was hardly seventeen, Peter was never able to forgive or forget his forced transfer to the cold capital where he had to speak a strange language and profess a new faith. To make things worse, Grand Duke Pyotr Feodorovich was married not to a young lady of his choice but to one chosen for him by Frederick II of Prussia and approved by Elizabeth of Russia. The lady was Princess Sophie of Anhalt-Zerbst, a member of a small, princely family whose father, Prince Christian Augustus, served in the Prussian army and whose mother was a social climber, Princess Johanna Elizabeth of Holstein. In August, 1745, Princess Sophie too embraced Orthodoxy, and was renamed Catherine, to be known later as Catherine II. The bridegroom was hardly seventeen, the bride sixteen years of age.

**Peter and Catherine.** A more incompatible marital union could not be imagined—the two conflicted in every respect. Nature lavishly endowed Catherine with many attractive qualities; but it was most scant in the case of her husband Peter. Physically, Peter was most unattractive and was handicapped mentally as well. He was indeed such a total ignoramus that he shocked even Elizabeth, who was by no means erudite. He was conceited, contentious, capricious, and stubborn, while Catherine possessed a great deal of personal charm, vivacity, intelligence, and astuteness. The only reason for her consent to such an incongruous union, it may be assumed, was her hidden ambition to wear someday the crown that ill fit her husband. (*See Reading No. 7.*)

Even in his early youth Peter demonstrated an inability or unwillingness to exert his mental faculties. For this reason his tutors employed visual aids, such as profusely illustrated books, coins, and medals that registered dates and named heroes. Occasionally they would use the globe, but Peter showed little interest in geography. In one field only did he display any sign of excitement—namely, in military science—though even here he manifested a rather superficial curiosity. He considered the most important date in military history the day he was raised from a non-commissioned officer to the rank of major. When Peter donned the Prussian-like uniform he himself designed, he must have provoked many a secret laugh: the uniform was so tight it made him look like a ramrod, and the enormous hat would fall down his small head to make him look like a pathetic marionette. Small wonder that the troops during the frequent parades could hardly control themselves.

In 1754 Catherine gave birth to a son named Paul whose maternity was more certain than his paternity. Be that as it may, officially Paul became the legitimate heir to the Russian throne. Elizabeth could rejoice for she felt that the genealogical continuity had now been secured. Meanwhile, both parents led their own lives apart from each other. Peter frankly cursed his lot and the country foisted upon him; he amused himself with dolls and wax or lead soldiers, and court-martialled trapped rats. Catherine, at the same time, shrewdly cultivated devotees who some day might be instrumental in state affairs, studied Russian, professed loyalty to her recently adopted country, and carefully studied the art of statesmanship. While Catherine gained admirers among native Russian court members, Peter associated himself mainly with those Baltic Germans who unhesitatingly demonstrated Prussophile sentiments and were openly contemptuous of Russia. Frederick II gambled on the complaisant German element that surrounded Peter while he was engaged in his war on all fronts.

By the end of 1761, Prussia's fate seemed in the balance and it looked as if divine Providence alone could come to the rescue of the "old rascal," Frederick II. On

January 5, 1762, Elizabeth died and events suddenly took a different turn: the implacable foe of Prussia was replaced by an enthusiastic admirer. Before her death Elizabeth had been somewhat disturbed by the German intrigues at court and the unfavorable reports from the front. The growing influence of the men who surrounded Peter III, the heir Elizabeth herself had chosen, must have been a source of melancholy to her. Only death precluded her schemes to forestall a possible shift in the alignment against Prussia.

**The Short Reign of Peter III.** Upon Elizabeth's death, according to her will, the throne passed to her nephew, Peter III, who immediately reversed the diplomatic allegiance of Russia to Austria. As a pathological Prussophile he ordered immediate withdrawal from the war, an act which comforted Frederick II as much as it distressed patriotic Russians. By a single stroke every recent potential gain was wiped out, while Frederick II was saved from what had seemed his inevitable doom. In domestic affairs also the six-month reign of Peter III proved momentous.

**Emancipation of the Nobility.** The outstanding act of Peter III was his issuing of the Manifesto of February 1762, freeing the nobility from all obligatory service to the state, though retaining the laws that exacted service from the peasantry. This marked the crowning victory of the Russian nobility. Whereas formerly land was granted in return for service to the state, now it was given in perpetuity, with the owners being allowed to retain absolute mastery over their serfs. Land and serf ownership became an exclusive privilege of the nobility. The class became henceforth a more corporate caste, closing its ranks almost completely against outsiders.

Some of the decrees issued during the short reign of Peter III produced the outward impression of royal magnanimity and liberal intent. Such was the granting of religious freedom to the Old Believers and the abolition of the secret police. Yet their true aim was merely to ingratiate the new sovereign with his people and minimize the implications of the February Manifesto. And still, as was expected, the February Manifesto aroused much resentment among the peasantry. The scheme to secularize the land that belonged to religious institutions simultaneously aroused the clergy. The military innovations, all aping the Prussian system, antagonized the high-ranking officers in the armed forces. The return of the Baltic Germans into prominence at court and in the army offended national feelings. As if this were not enough, there came a rumor that Peter III contemplated wresting Schleswig from Denmark even if it required a declaration of war. It was amidst this growing discontent, and the prevailing fear of a new war in which Russia would have no interest whatever, that Catherine was able to gain popularity among the Guards. She masterfully prepared the ground by ingratiating herself with them, by gaining to her side the necessary influential people, and by posing as a patriot and the unhappy wife of a mentally deranged and misguided sovereign. Such was the atmosphere in July, 1762, when the plot was being contrived.

**Peter III Leaves an Impact Upon Russia.** The impact the brief reign of Peter III had upon foreign affairs was no less profound in the field of domestic developments. A thumbnail sketch of what took place in Russian foreign relations during the preceding decades seems necessary. From 1725, the year of Peter I's death, to 1762, the year of Catherine's ascendancy, Russia became irretrievably involved in the system of continental diplomacy. The immediate few years following Peter I's reign enabled the people to recover from his tumultuous quarter of a century. Soon after Anne came to power Russia found herself supporting Augustus III of Poland, who at considerable Russian expense was crowned in 1734. Hardly recovered from the war of the Polish Succession, Russia in 1736 plunged into another war with Turkey over the Crimean Tartars who continued to raid the northern borders and cause untold devastation to Russian communities. Despite a successful campaign and high sacrifices the Treaty of Belgrade in 1739 denied Russia her main goal, an outlet to the Black Sea.

**Russia and the Seven Years' War.** Since 1726 Russia had had an alliance with Austria which had brought her nothing but grief. For one thing, the alliance was instrumental in causing Russian participation in the Seven Years' War against Prussia. The campaign in August, 1757, augured signs of success as the army invaded

Prussia and continued to move onward, but suddenly, for no clear reason, an order was issued to halt the offensive. There was strong suspicion that this was the work of the pro-Prussian elements, who took advantage of Elizabeth's incapacity. The more likely it seemed that Peter might assume power, the bolder became the conduct of the pro-Prussian elements at court. To their disappointment Elizabeth managed to recover from the stroke and the campaign in East Prussia was renewed with vigor.

Early in 1758 the Russian army launched an offensive, swiftly moving into Königsberg while Frederick was desperately fighting on other fronts. By the middle of the summer the invading army reached Küstrin and started to move toward Berlin. Late in August Frederick II dashed madly to halt the enemy from the east. A stalemate ensued, accompanied by occasional flashes of hope, one of which was the successful raid on Berlin early in October (8-11). But the war dragged on until early in 1762, with the Russian army bogged down in Pomerania. The Prussian army simultaneously reached a state of complete exhaustion, best demonstrated by Frederick's readiness to sue for peace. It was at this turn of events that Frederick II received the news that Elizabeth had died and that to the throne had come his admirer Peter III. Nothing could have been more pleasing to Frederick at this grave hour than the news from St. Petersburg. Although the war was continued by the Allies until 1763, ending with the *status quo ante bellum,* Frederick II did manage to retain Silesia. Peter III's first step, withdrawal from the war, saved his Prussian King, but also sent him toward his own doom and assisted the rise of Catherine II to power.

**The Overthrow of Peter III.** The rising national protest against a sovereign who pursued policies damaging to state interests constituted the background of the court revolution in 1762. The revolt could have been carried out in favor of two legitimate claimants: Ivan VI, who was lingering in prison, or Paul, the eight-year-old son of Catherine. Neither name was even mentioned, since the chief figure on stage was Catherine herself. At the time of the plot Catherine was in Peterhof, a suburb of the capital, where she was to be joined by her husband. Peter intended to spend a short while there and then return to St. Petersburg to witness the departure of troops to Holstein. At the moment the plot was to be carried out Peter III was at a party at Oranienbaum. Meanwhile, Catherine, aided by a group of her favorites, was forced to act with haste for at the last moment she thought the plot might be uncovered. As soon as she was assured of the support of Guards, Senate, and Synod, there remained little else but to proclaim herself Empress of Russia. Having accomplished her goal on July 8, 1762, the Empress returned to Peterhof.

**End of Peter III.** When rumors gradually reached Peter about his wife's plotting, he dispatched messengers to the capital to persuade Catherine to abandon her scheme. The messengers, however, only joined the cause of the plotters. Peter, meanwhile, remained deserted at Oranienbaum until the next day, when he had no choice but to sign the abdication. After he attached his signature he was transferred to the nearby village of Ropsha, where he was placed under special guard. The official account states that a week after his arrival, a party was held during which there was much festivity, drinking, and political argument. One of the debates led to a brawl in which Peter presumably was killed by accident. (*See Readings Nos. 8 and 9.*)

— 6 —

# THE REIGN OF CATHERINE II,
### 1762-96

**Her Ascendancy.** Before Catherine was able to carry out her plot successfully she had to quash three legitimate claimants: one was her husband, Peter III, another was Ivan VI, still kept in the Schlüsselburg fortress, and the third was her own eight-year-old son, Paul. This she accomplished with skillful efficiency and dispatch. The long reign of Catherine II may be historically regarded as a second chapter in the Petrine era. If the reign of Peter demolished the Muscovite order, the reign of Catherine II marked the definite formation of the St. Petersburg order. Metaphorically speaking, Peter I cultivated the soil, and Catherine II gathered the harvest. It must be borne in mind that by the time Catherine II reached the helm of power not only had a new generation risen within the Petrine atmosphere, but also a small elite minority steeped in the new ideas. Nor must it be forgotten that by Catherine's time the nobility had managed to free itself from obligatory service, while serf labor was tied down more than ever to the masters' estates. The landed gentry had tasted the fruits of freedom, the advantages derived from exploitation of serf labor, and the comforts of extravagant living at home or abroad. Furthermore, by a fortunate coincidence, Poland and Turkey were then on the decline, thereby affording new power to Russia, their traditional contestant.

**Personality of Catherine.** Let us first take a closer look at Catherine II, the woman who came to rule the country for some thirty-four years. Catherine was fortunate in one respect—to have as her predecessor Peter III, and her successor Paul I. When people compared their reigns with Catherine's hers would seem indeed an era of a perfect rule. Contemporaries and those who cherished memories of the "Catherine Days" were able, shortly after her reign, to create a legendary tale which ran somewhat as follows: here was a poor German princess of Anhalt-Zerbst, who had every honorable intention of serving her adopted country and people, yet was persecuted by a half-wit husband. Tormented as a wife, tested as a patriot, she finally succeeded in casting off the intolerable burden and assumed power for the greater glory of the Russian Empire. There was no denying that her reign marked the attainment of an old national dream of control over the Black Sea shores and the elimination of Russia's traditional rival—Poland.

The first impression one obtained when meeting this Russian Semiramis was her physical vigor and bursting energy. Though not beautiful, Catherine had a command-

ing dignity of gait and on official occasions, when she
would make her appearance in all regalia, the sight was
so impressive that it commanded respect even from her
foes. Her large forehead, Roman nose, excellent teeth
that stood out prominently when she smiled, the warmth
in her eyes, her extraordinarily white skin—these seemed
to be the features noted by most of those who knew
Catherine personally. Her proud bearing and the manner
in which she spoke or appeared during parades and
official receptions betrayed an air of royalty. Her ingratiating manner of speech gained her many admirers. Self-
taught, Catherine proved to be such an extremely cultured
woman that she impressed many western European intellectual leaders of the eighteenth century. She read prodi-
giously, and her book collection included both ancient
and modern literature.

That Catherine merited the power she seized is not
doubted. Nature endowed her with a keen mind which,
as one observer aptly remarked, was noted more for its
width and length than for its depth. She could quickly
seize ideas expressed by others, synthesize them, and
derive deductions in a manner that would bring down
the tablets of wisdom from abstract heights to the level
of concrete thinking. Her eclectic mind could absorb
ideas emanating from many sources, then choose what
she preferred and add a touch of her own. For this reason
most of her ideas can be easily traced to their original
sources. Catherine's gift, as she herself knew, was for
synthesis rather than creation.

Catherine was noted for her adaptability to various
conditions and for her ability to calculate political and
diplomatic moves with frigid detachment. Yet her buoy-
ant nature and her passionate love of men, bordering at
times on sensuality, revealed a degree of romantic loneli-
ness. Affectation was alien to her and for this reason
Catherine disliked pseudoclassical literature, particularly
tragedies. She hated pomposity and urged writers not to
belabor style but rather to be precise and brief. Style,
like humor, she maintained, must be as natural as breath-
ing. Music never seemed to have any appeal to Catherine,
most likely because that art involves a degree of mysticism which had always been alien to her. She possessed
a rational mind, at times almost too calculating to appre-

ciate the pure arts. Catherine was almost always pre-occupied and, as she herself once said, "By nature I love to work and the more I work the happier I am." She admitted herself that she never had any system and only one ambition—the welfare of the state. Much of what Catherine was trying to accomplish politically had been calculated to cultivate national pride at home or to command respect abroad. Social injustice and economic hardships were to be overshadowed by dazzling glories and territorial expansion. For this reason court life during her reign frequently assumed glittering colors, with many commemorations of military victories and other festivities; an extensive program for the construction of public buildings was undertaken; museums and academies received generous support to impress opinion abroad.

**Political Ideas.** Catherine tried ardently to raise the nation to a higher cultural level, and it must be admitted that she herself studied and wrote more than any one else within the Empire. She wittily contended that while writing in Russian her use of wrong cases could harm no one, yet her writings might serve today to educate a large number of people and add prestige to literature. Public education she regarded as a step toward national enlightenment, which in turn would mean justice, tolerance, and public welfare. Montesquieu's *Spirit of the Laws* Catherine regarded as the prayerbook of monarchs. In later years Catherine, as the product of her *Zeitgeist,* learned to her chagrin that traditions have deeper roots than her rationalistic blueprints; prevailing conditions in the country made her philosophical journeys into the future rather hazardous. As she came to probe conditions without the aid of the Encyclopedists and arrive at more realistic conclusions, Catherine had to shed her former theories. In the end she revealed her purple rather than red banner, championing the cause of divine right and exerting all efforts to save whatever possible from the wreckage of the French Revolution.

**Internal Affairs.** Shortly after her ascendancy Catherine II summoned a Legislative Commission to consider the codification of the laws. In 1766 some 658 deputies assembled, a colorful array representing every class, race, and garb of every part of the Empire. The Empress had drafted a special "Instruction" for the deputies, which she compiled from current writings of the Encyclopedists. The Commission started with great fanfare and sat for many months discussing matters, but with few constructive results; under the pretext of the forthcoming war, which broke out in 1768, the assembly was prorogued, never to be summoned again.

The old administrative division instituted by Peter I proved awkward. Catherine redivided the country into fifty instead of the former ten gubernias, thereby improving local administration considerably. It was also under Catherine II that the monastic estates were secularized. Much was done under her direction to colonize the recently acquired southern territories; German farmers were encouraged to settle some sections, thus forming colonies that prevailed until recent times. It was under her direction also that public welfare was first established, largely in the form of orphanages, schools, and hospitals. The Ukraine fared poorly during Catherine's reign, since the Cossacks who refused to yield their old rights migrated southeast. Ukrainian autonomy declined rapidly: the office of the Hetman was abolished and with it all vestiges of former liberties. During the second half of the eighteenth century literary writings and early Russian journalism made their appearance. Among the outstanding publishers was Novikov, who, however, ended sadly, as did one of the distinguished writers of her time, Radishchev, author of the famed *Journey from St. Petersburg to Moscow,* in which he attacked the institution of serfdom. It was most unfortunate that at the time these men became eminent in national life developments in France assumed such character that Catherine became frightened by new ideas. Any progressive scheme to alter the social structure was now interpreted as Jacobinism. However, the most outstanding development remained the emancipated nobility that now came to play a more decisive part in national life than ever before. This class, after winning its freedom, managed to draw up a special charter, stipulating succinctly the privileges it had sought long ago, and now succeeded in having it sanctioned by the Crown. For further security the privileges now became part of the laws of the land.

**External Affairs: Turkey.** It is in external affairs that the reign of Catherine II stands out particularly. By a strange conjuncture it so happened that an Empress of German extraction succeeded in achieving what no Russian sovereign had managed since the sixteenth century. One circumstance was the war with Turkey of 1768-74, which ended with the significant treaty of Kuchuk Kainardji; the other was the dismemberment of Poland. This forced Russia into the arena of continental diplomacy as never before and subsequently brought her to grief. By the treaty of Kuchuk Kainardji, signed on July 21, 1774, Russia gained relatively little territory. The potentialities of the treaty were more important than any territorial gains. One of the stipulations granted independence to the Crimean Khanate, which shortly afterward led to an outright incorporation of the peninsula into the Russian Empire. The other and more significant provision was the right of protectorship given to Russia over Orthodox Christians within the Turkish Empire. Henceforth, for more than three-quarters of a century, Russia, basing her actions on treaty rights, kept intervening in the internal affairs of Turkey and so undermining the Empire.

Poland. In the case of Poland the situation was different. Here the long rivalry between the two Slavic states led to the final collapse of the weaker. The sorrowful end of Poland was caused partly by her lack of political stability and diplomatic acumen, and partly by outside conniving, largely by Frederick II, with the half-hearted consent of Catherine II. During the first partition, Maria Theresa shed a tear over the lot of Poland but nontheless took her fat share of the spoils. By the first partition of 1772 (performed by Prussia, Russia, and Austria), the second in 1793 (by Prussia and Russia only), and the third in 1795 (by the former three again), Poland as a state vanished from the map of the Continent. The new division established a common border between Russia, Prussia, and Austria, and Russia at last settled her scores with her age-old opponent. But if Russia succeeded in destroying the national state she failed to destroy the nation. By partitioning the country Russia extended westward not only a portion of territory predominantly settled by Poles, thereby including a turbulent national minority, but also incorporated Lithuania and the Duchy of Courland, long contested areas. The territorial acquisition perpetuated further the deep-seated enmity that poisoned relations between the two states and created a legacy still felt in eastern Europe.

**The End.** Catherine II started as a liberal, toyed with ideas that often baffled her ministers in St. Petersburg, and gained admirers in Paris. But as the years went by she revealed the purple color of her liberalism. The Pugachev rebellion frightened her and the French revolution turned into a haunting nightmare. If Catherine was incapable of wreaking vengeance on revolutionary France she found more successful outlets in Poland, where she could claim suppression of Jacobinism, and in Turkey, where she could begin a crusade on behalf of Christian civilization. She hoped next, after her victories in Poland and Turkey, to incorporate the Caucasus, but death precluded her from completing the plan.

The death of Catherine II, in November, 1796, ended a checkered era of glory marred by events foreboding graver consequences. The advance in the south was to her credit as a step toward civilization; the advance in the west across the corpse of the Polish state, the privileges showered on the nobility, and the grinding down of the peasantry left a legacy which successive generations had to pay for rather dearly.

— 7 —

# THE REIGN OF PAUL I, 1796-1801

**Personality of Paul.** For the remaining four years of the eighteenth century Russia came under the rule of one of the most colorful of royal personalities, Paul I. He was born in 1754 and at the time of his ascendancy was forty-two years of age. In her Memoirs Catherine refers to the alienation between herself and her son Paul caused by Elizabeth. Yet after Elizabeth's death Catherine did little to correct the situation. She seldom saw her son and rarely manifested any maternal affection toward the boy. Since Paul was the legitimate claimant to the throne Catherine feared him and for this reason conveniently made him reside in the nearby town of Gatchina.

In due course the relationship between Catherine and Paul deteriorated into bitter hostility that deepened as the years went by. From his very childhood Catherine showed unconcealed doubts as to Paul's native intelligence or ability to learn anything, and he was deprived of any activities that might have afforded him normal development. His physical appearance did little to impress people: he was short, unattractive, and nervous, and from an early age had trouble with his lymphatic gland. The care of Paul was casual to say the least. Catherine entrusted the youth to Count N. I. Panin as tutor and thenceforth cared little whether the pupil studied or made any progress at all. It was no surprise that the tutoring proved inadequate; as one of Paul's later tutors observed, it seemed as if the main purpose of his training was to cultivate in him a revulsion rather than an interest in the fields of study.

Nor can much be said about Paul's general upbringing —it hardly contributed to an ennobling of his character. His formative years seemed to have been devoted to deforming him, yet there is no evidence whatever that his unbearable character was due to inborn traits. On the contrary, in his earlier days Paul demonstrated a keen interest in books, especially in the field of mathematics. On various occasions he proved himself to possess an alert and receptive mind. It was most unfortunate that this rather promising youth was deprived of the opportunity to grow up normally under sympathetic care. The sting of dour resentment against a lost childhood wasted outside the capital must have scarred his character for the rest of his life.

**A Family Entanglement.** In Paul's lifetime one may find no more than two or three bright moments. One was in 1772, when for a brief period his relations with his mother promised to become friendlier because Orlov, one of Catherine's prominent favorites whom Paul detested, ceased his courtship. Another was his first short-lived marriage (1773-76) contracted, incidentally, without Catherine's consent. The marital union seemed to have mellowed Paul. A third episode might be included, Paul's second marriage to a woman who, from all evidence, understood Paul well and did everything possible to stand up against his reverses in life. Yet even at this seemingly promising turn of events normal family life was excruciatingly difficult. For one thing, Catherine asserted her right to take their children under her own protective wing, as Elizabeth had done when she took Peter III under her personal care. Catherine showed extreme solicitude toward her most favored grandchild, Alexander. For this Paul could never forgive his mother, and henceforth not only did he resent his mother's interference with parental duties, but he suspected, and rightly so, political motivation: Paul feared that both his mother and son were scheming to bar him from assuming power and to will the throne to Alexander. Fear and suspicion made him erratic, totally unreasonable, and unpredictable. His daily decrees later were confusing, repetitious, or entirely contradictory. Neither age nor rank could spare anyone from the raging fury which Paul let loose in public. Absolutism reached its apogee. Once, to combat widespread administrative abuses in the country Paul ordered that a box be installed in front of the Winter Palace, the key of which he kept himself. Here any subject might leave whatever complaint he had or report any abuses known to him. A few weeks later the box was removed, since instead of complaints people started to drop satirical verses and caricatures of the Emperor himself.

Paul's lonely and abnormal boyhood and early manhood was caused also by political apprehension: The moment someone became closely associated with Paul his mother would see to his removal for fear that a plot might be in the making. Even his own son Alexander, Catherine kept away from Paul under the pretext of bringing up her darling grandson as the future "enlightened sovereign." All this led Paul to believe that his son, too, had been plotting against his legitimate claim to the throne. Altogether it produced an atmosphere charged with suspicion, resentment, and thirst for vengeance, as well as the peculiar situation in which association with Paul carried with it an aura of disloyalty to Catherine; on the other hand, those who enjoyed favors at court were regarded as potential foes of Paul.

The "Little Court" at Gatchina. Confined to his provincial residence at Gatchina, Paul rarely travelled even in his own country. His enforced idleness afforded him time for frequent contemplation of his lot; in the end he turned morose and bitter against his mother and her courtiers in the capital. The isolation at Gatchina distorted Paul's character and left him with an acid resentment that deepened with the years of awaiting the day he would be able to reassert and vindicate himself. Because of his isolated life Paul became uncommunicative, unsociable, and awkward in company or on official occasions. The long years prior to his ascendancy developed in him a distrust of men, and an irritable disposition which often expressed itself in ugly outbursts of anger followed by profound melancholy. Paul sought solace in religious faith, yet it failed to give him complete peace of mind; frequent moments of hope would be followed by periods of despair and anguish. His conduct would become uncontrollable, unpredictable, politically dangerous.

Nor did his life at Gatchina offer him any intellectual stimulation. Petty details of daily routine preoccupied his existence. The "Little Court" distorted everything, reduced life to minutiae. Here Paul was in charge of a military unit that counted some two thousand strong. Not being able to extend his vision beyond petty issues Paul was compelled to stress such aspects of army life as drill perfection, manner of step, or type of uniform. For the same reason Paul came to emphasize the importance of parades, which became almost a daily affair, and later to carry this parade mania to the capital. Since Paul had never been given the opportunity to participate in any military campaign, with the exception of a very brief visit to the Swedish front, he never acquired any true sense of military perception. The cumulative effect of all this was that by the time Paul reached the throne his conduct was that of a pathologically sick man haunted by all sorts of fantastic visions. He alienated everybody and wondered why no one admired him. His wife once sadly predicted that Paul might end up a victim at the hands of his own subjects. Looking as his four-year reign one gains the impression of a man furiously driving himself toward his own tragic end.

**Domestic Affairs.** Being nearly deprived of the crown, Paul, shortly after his accession to the throne, ordered that the law of succession be altered or made more precise. On April 16, 1797, he decreed that henceforth the crown must pass from father to the eldest son. This clarified the law and made circumvention more difficult. Simultaneously, Paul issued a Manifesto which forbade the use of serf labor on Sundays and in excess of three days weekly. In some parts of the country, where the landlords required not more than two days a week, the law caused more confusion than restraint.

Almost from the very start Paul stripped all Catherine's recent favorites of the privileges so generously lavished upon them. Many of them were compelled to leave the capital, and their places were taken by those whose loyalty had been tested by Paul at Gatchina. In one of his vindictive fits Paul revoked the charters which his mother had granted to the nobility and to the municipalities. This act nearly wrecked the system of local government which the preceding reign had successfully established.

Paul sadly lacked dignity or poise and frequently displayed terrific outbursts of ill-controlled temper. Yet he insisted upon absolute control over every phase of national administration, be it of imperial or local nature. The result was a capricious despotism often motivated by petty vindictiveness. When, for instance, the peasants came in conflict with their masters over the exact interpretation of the three-day-a-week serf labor, which presumably was to defend the interests of the peasants, Paul suppressed with extreme harshness any sign of discontent on the part of the peasants. The gentry Paul regarded as reliable local police officers throughout the Empire and granted them powers accordingly. Furthermore, to win their loyalty and for the sake of public order as envisioned by Paul, he light-heartedly transferred to the gentry an enormous amount of land owned by the state and with it over a half million formerly free peasants who would now become serfs. During his four-year reign Paul transferred to the gentry almost two-thirds as many peasants as did Catherine II during her whole thirty-four years.

**Church and State.** Equally inconsistent was Paul's

policy concerning the church. Paul showed surprising tolerance toward dissenters, including the Old Believers, and granted them the right to conduct their religious services publicly. The clergy was seriously disturbed by such leniency. More embarrassing was Paul's practice of bestowing medals upon high clerics. The church frowned upon such a practice but was unable to do much about it. Further confusion ensued when Paul accepted the title of Grand Master of the Order of Knights of St. John and thereby assumed protectorship of the organization. It was indeed strange that a Russian sovereign who was regarded as head of the Orthodox faith simultaneously assumed the headship of an Order that was subordinate to the Pope of Rome.

**Tyranny in Action.** If some of Paul's policies were baffling because of their absolute inconsistency or contradictions, others were outright tyrannical. Publication of books and periodicals came to a virtual standstill and books printed abroad were banned throughout the country. Travel in foreign countries was forbidden and aliens were barred from entry into Russia. As a Frankophobe Paul objected to any French importation, whether it be books, pictures, or Parisian-tailored clothes. Into the army he introduced an iron discipline that caused much discontent among all ranks for its senseless harshness and total futility. Endless parades was the order of the day. These were to be carried out in uniforms designed by Paul himself, which were more fitting for a ballet corps than a military regiment.

**External Policy.** Even more bewildering was Paul's conduct in external affairs. Shortly before Catherine's death Russia joined the war against France, but as soon as Paul came to power he declared that Russia was in no condition to render active military assistance. Then, just as suddenly, in 1799, Paul rejoined the coalition against Napoleon and ordered an army headed by Russia's illustrious general Suvorov, to join the Austrians against France in northern Italy and later in Switzerland. The campaign in Italy proved successful, but in Switzerland Suvorov encountered serious reverses caused chiefly by topographic and military impediments. After much hardship, and with extraordinary valor, Suvorov managed to retreat across the Alps into southern Germany, ascribing his plight to insufficient aid from Austria. Paul, in a characteristic outburst of temper, terminated the alliance in 1800 and severed relations with Austria. Shortly afterwards, a similar complaint of inadequate cooperation with a Russian force in Holland caused Paul to sever relations with England.

**Paul and Napoleon.** This feuding among the allies gave Napoleon an excellent opportunity to win the fickle Paul to his side. He promised to give Russia the island of Malta where, at the moment, a French force was under siege by the English. Another gesture of magnanimity was Napoleon's order to free all Russian war prisoners in France without requesting the customary ransom. The game proved successful: Paul was charmed by Napoleon not only as a person but as a statesman and the savior of France. Within a short time Russia and France reached a peaceful settlement and Paul concluded an alliance with Prussia against Austria, and another with Denmark and Sweden against England. English ships were seized in Russian ports, and at Napoleon's instigation Paul schemed to seize India. But a war with England was the last thing either the Russian army or the gentry wished since it would be undesirable from a military point of view as well as economically hazardous.

**The Violent End.** The growing discontent against Paul's muddled policies made him only more contentious and unpredictable. He developed an almost pathological fear of plots against himself and was continually haunted by a suspicion that he might share the fate of his father, Peter III. His constant suspicion resulted in wider persecutions, which included even members of his own family. Finally the situation became so unbearable that a group of courtiers decided to request his abdication. A small group of plotters, headed by Nikita Panin and motivated by patriotic devotion to the country, decided to act quickly and vigorously. In order to strengthen their cause morally, they induced Grand Duke Alexander to join them, promising him that his father would suffer no violence. Whether Panin became suspect or for other reasons, he was forced to depart from the capital. His place was taken by Count Pahlen, who was even more determined to settle matters and rid the country of the royal madman.

During the night of March 23, 1801, the conspirators forced their way into the imperial bed chamber and demanded that Paul sign his abdication. As was anticipated, Paul violently refused to comply with the request. A scuffle ensued and Paul was strangled. Next day the throne passed to Alexander I, Paul's eldest son, who was deeply moved by the preceding events and who often blamed himself for his father's tragic end.

— 8 —

# THE REIGN OF ALEXANDER I, 1801-25

**Personality of Alexander I.** The personality of the "enigmatic tsar" has fascinated many writers. Yet upon closer examination the character of Alexander seems no more enigmatic than that of many others of his time. The first quarter of the nineteenth century had an ominous beginning and an equally ominous finale: it started with the strangulation of Paul I and ended with cannon shots on the Senate Square, suppressing the Decembrist revolt. Such were the prologue and epilogue of the reign of Alexander I.

**Education and Marriage.** The new sovereign was born in St. Petersburg on December 24, 1777. His first tutor was General N. I. Saltykov, a fawning courtier who assumed the unenviable role of go-between for the grandmother and parents of the pupil. In 1784, hardly seven years of age, Alexander was assigned to a Swiss tutor, F. C. Laharpe, who was requested to speak to the boy only in French. The new tutor had at that time strong republican proclivities and liberal ideas, with which he imbued Alexander. A certain A. A. Samborski who had

married an English woman, dressed in secular attire, and
had a clean shaven face, was called to court to teach
Alexander religion. Laharpe was a typical product of the
eighteenth century, a rationalist who, like Catherine, must
have taken on his assignment as a mission to "enlighten"
the future monarch of Russia. Yet the environment in
which Alexander grew up was hardly conducive either to
enlightenment or to rational thought. Endless intrigues,
family antagonism, subservience, and favoritism hardly
inspired one to poised contemplation.

In 1793 Alexander, then fifteen, and Louise, fourteen-
year-old daughter of the Prince of Baden, announced their
engagement, and were married that same year in October.
(Characteristically, the announcement itself served to
antagonize the family: Alexander was assigned a much
larger court staff than his father had, something Paul
failed neither to notice nor to forgive.) Alexander's early
marriage terminated further schooling; whatever he subsequently learned was entirely from observation or experience. Considering his short inadequate training, it is
surprising how much Alexander did learn. (*See Reading
No. 10.*)

His early life was torn between the two worlds symbolized by the Winter Palace and Gatchina; between the
sweet reasoning of Laharpe and the sullenness of his
father; between the glitter of the court at St. Petersburg
and the gray, barrackslike atmosphere of the "Little
Court" of Gatchina. Basically, Alexander had an unhappy childhood and must have been at heart an unhappy
man. His father's tragic end, to which Alexander indirectly consented, made little change in his already sad
disposition. The care of his grandmother had deprived
him from his youth of parental affection.

**Father and Son.** Under the watchful eye of Catherine II, Alexander dared not show any attachment to
his father, which infuriated Paul. The entire situation was
fraught with misunderstanding and suspicion, which led
to an exchange of hypocritical pleasantries in an atmosphere of strain and stress. As early as 1791 Catherine had
contemplated stripping Paul of his right to succession;
three years later she announced her intention to the State
Council. Both Paul and Alexander were fully aware of
this, and whereas one was full of helpless fury the other

simply stood by passively. Since Laharpe was not in favor
of Catherine's plan he was soon removed, and after a
short audience with Paul in the spring of 1795 he de-
parted for western Europe. Before the two separated
Laharpe implored Paul to be friendly with Alexander,
to deal with him directly and treat him kindly. During
the ensuing separation Alexander corresponded with his
former tutor and adviser. In one of his letters Alexander
raises a corner of the curtain to reveal some of his inner
torment. He stated that he contemplated abdication because the surrounding atmosphere was intolerable, that
it was difficult to locate an honest man. Furthermore, he
hoped to employ his absolute power in order to establish
a representative form of government. After having accomplished this mission, Alexander hoped to settle down
somewhere along the Rhine where, amidst bucolic scen-
ery, he could spent the rest of his life in private retire-
ment. But fate had prepared a different future for him.

When Alexander came to power his experience was
limited, to say the least. Born in St. Petersburg, residing
most of his life among alien people, always under the
influence of foreign developments and foreign thought,
Alexander had little knowledge of his own country except
for its negative characteristics. From his grandmother he
inherited a love for imperial splendor; from his father he
learned to admire military parades. He never received
any disciplinary schooling, not even an elementary one;
he had neither the time nor the desire to study. Yet the
urgent state of affairs in which Russia had found herself
at the time of his accession compelled Alexander to learn
fast. The immediate effect of the young sovereign was
the prevention of an Anglo-Russian conflict. The first
thing Alexander did was to order the Cossack detachment
to the Indian border to be returned home; at the same
time he assured England of his peaceful intentions.
Having averted war between England and Russia Alexander next turned to no less urgent problems at home.

The Early Council. One of the first things Alexander
did was to call upon a small group of young men to
serve in an advisory capacity. These young men, very
much like Alexander himself, had more youthful zeal
than practical ability. One of the issues that increasingly
concerned them was that of serfdom. After rather lengthy

discussion the government declared in 1803 that it would favor emancipation of the serfs provided the conditions were arrived at privately between landlord and serfs and each contract was officially approved before going into effect. The decree failed dismally, but at least it proved that the institution of serfdom urgently demanded serious attention. Yet external events soon followed which overshadowed all domestic affairs and forced the government to concentrate on developments in Western Europe.

**Precarious Neutrality.** From the preceding reign Alexander inherited a complex legacy of foreign bungling that threatened the country with war. At first there was a serious possibility of war with England which only the strangling of Paul precluded. After forestalling this conflict, Alexander hoped to maintain a neutral position for the time being in order to bring about badly needed domestic reforms. But while relations with England showed immediate improvement those with France did not. Napoleon's position of domination on the continent compelled Alexander to seek closer ties with Austria and England; when these two states became engaged in a war with France in 1805, Russia's neutral position became untenable and soon she joined the Third Coalition. That the country was in no condition to participate in a continental conflict was soon discovered, though at a rather costly price.

**Russia at War.** With lightning speed Napoleon struck Austria, occupied Vienna, and early in December, 1805, delivered a smashing defeat to the combined Austro-Russian armies at Austerlitz. Austria sued for peace, the Russian army retreated eastward, and Napoleon moved next against Prussia. By the middle of October, 1806, the Prussians were defeated at Jena; at the end of the month Napoleon triumphantly entered Berlin, and then moved on to East Prussia and Poland, where he was enthusiastically welcomed. By midsummer, 1807, Russia found herself alone facing a victorious Napoleon. England was of little help and could not be counted upon as an effective ally. Alexander, having no choice, dourly consented to seek a peaceful settlement with Napoleon. The two Emperors met at Tilsit, where the peace was signed. According to the Treaty of Tilsit, Russia lost none of her territory, but she lost her allies and more than that. She was compelled either to see that England made peace with France or else to join the Continental Blockade. Furthermore, in addition to the humiliation of Prussia, Alexander had to accept the creation of the Duchy of Warsaw formed out of the territories Prussia had obtained as a result of the second and third partitions of Poland. Alexander's only gain at Tilsit was that the former state of Poland would not be restored. In addition, Russia was given a free hand against Sweden and Turkey.

The Tilsit Peace. The war between France and Russia was fought on neither French nor Russian soil; neither side, therefore, suffered from either occupation or physical destruction. Nonetheless, the conflict left visible scars that required long-term healing. In the first place, Russia was entirely stripped of her allies and left alone to face Napoleon who dominated the continent of Europe. By virtue of Prussian defeat the French came uncomfortably closer to the borders of Russia. Furthermore, the formation of the Duchy of Warsaw was obviously meant, from its very inception, to serve as a weapon against Russia. It must also be borne in mind that the treaty of Tilsit stipulated Russia's joining the Continental Blockade. The severance of Anglo-Russian economic ties was a serious blow to Russia and caused much discontent among those mainly affected—the landed nobility. Short as the war was, it nevertheless caused a serious financial drain upon the country which in turn resulted in a postwar inflation of the currency, increasing the tax burdens and causing a decline in foreign trade. Such were the problems Alexander faced during the first few years of his reign. Recalling the recent sad fate of his father, Alexander had good reason to be disturbed by the opposition in the country toward coöperation with Napoleon. The Tilsit Peace held out no immediate bright prospects.

War in the North. Shortly after the signing of the Treaty of Tilsit, Russia began to utilize the free hand Napoleon had given Alexander in regard to Sweden and Turkey. Accordingly, Russia requested that Sweden terminate her alliance with England; when the request was refused, Russian troops invaded Finland. The war was brief and decisive and by the Treaty of Fredrikshamm of September 17, 1809, Finland, including the strategic Aaland Islands, was ceded by Sweden to Russia. Finland was granted the status of a Grand Duchy and the Emperor assumed the title of hereditary Grand Duke of Finland. Greater attention was then given to Turkey, where religious and racial sentiments and economic interests fused into a single issue—a drive to secure unhindered exit from the Black Sea into the Mediterranean.

**War in the South.** With Turkey hostilities broke out earlier, in 1806, when a Russian army invaded Moldavia and Wallachia. At Tilsit, Alexander and Napoleon agreed on the partition of Turkey, with the one significant exception of Constantinople, which must be excluded from the Russian sphere. While Russia was at war with Sweden an armistice was observed in the south. With the end of the Swedish war and the incorporation of Finland, the war with Turkey was revived. The conflict proved of longer duration than was anticipated, and as diplomatic relations with France again grew strained, peace in the south became urgent and the fulfillment of originally set goals was postponed. On May 28, 1812, the Treaty of Bucharest was signed, limiting Russian gains to Bessarabia and allowing an extension of her border to the Prut River and to the mouth of the Danube. Moldavia and Wallachia were returned to Turkey, who promised them administrative reforms. If, however, Russia failed to accomplish her goals in the southwest, in the Caucasus circumstances proved more favorable. In accordance with the Treaty of Gulistan, signed in 1813, Persia ceded to Russia the regions of Georgia, Baku, and adjacent areas. These gains gave Russia extensive control, stretching from the shores of the Black Sea to the Caspian. It took, however, several more decades before an effective administration, public order, and peace were established among the discontented natives.

**Attempts at Reforms.** During the short period between the signing of the Treaty of Tilsit and the outbreak of the second war with France in 1812, Alexander tried once more to revive some of his plans for domestic reforms. On this occasion he requested his able assistant, Michael Speransky, to draft a constitutional plan based on projects they had formerly discussed. As a result Speransky presented what seemed the first concrete program for political reform in the country. The program implied the abolition of serfdom and the guarantee of civil rights. It suggested administrative reforms by improving local government and reorganizing the Cabinet and the Council of State. With the exception of the latter two, all Speransky's suggestions remained on paper because of the attention required by the impending foreign crisis.

**Speransky Makes his Exit.** In order to relieve the economic strain which Russia experienced as a result of the first war with France, Speransky urged stabilization of the currency by means of higher taxes and relaxation in the observance of the Continental Blockade. This would involve the opening of Russian ports to neutral ships regardless of the nature of cargo these might carry. Speransky also recommended higher duties on luxury articles. Some of these recommendations were adopted, but the political reforms met severe criticism and effective opposition at court. His opponents successfully spread the rumor that Speransky was a Frankophile and in the spring of 1812 he was compelled to leave the capital, thereby marking the end of the second effort of Alexander I to introduce reforms in Russia.

**The Impending Crisis.** The feeling of an impending conflict between Russia and France had been keenly sensed ever since peace was signed and it rapidly mounted during the ensuing months. Relations worsened during these strenuous years for several reasons. There was much displeasure with the inadequate diplomatic aid which Alexander pledged to render to Napoleon at Tilsit. Napoleon was equally unhappy at the lack of strict enforcement of the Continental Blockade as well as at the new tariff policy, which seemed to affect French trade in particular. Personal feelings between Alexander and Napoleon aggravated matters further when the former declined to give his consent to the marriage of his sister Ann to the French Emperor, who had recently divorced Josephine. Nor was Alexander himself entirely satisfied with the course of developments since 1807. He had good reasons to be disturbed by French intentions to revive the Polish state: it might serve to block Russian expansion and might become an ally of France. Furthermore, events made it increasingly clear that the insatiable territorial appetite of Napoleon was bound to lead to a state of affairs in which the French and Russian Empires would become incompatible as European powers. The inevitable crisis came in the summer of 1812.

**Invasion of Russia.** On June 24 Napoleon's Grand Army, about 620,000 strong, crossed the Niemen River and began to advance eastward. Although the conflict had been anticipated and Russia, to face the emergency, had hastily signed a peace treaty in the south, the army was hardly in condition to conduct war on a grand scale. For this reason Russia had chosen a strategy in depth, whereby the enemy would be enticed inland as far from his bases as possible, lengthening his lines of communication to a near breaking point. Then Russia would strike with all available resources. It was in this manner that Napoleon kept pressing toward his goal, Moscow, where he hoped to dictate peace terms. With the exception of a few blood-letting engagements which served to drain his manpower seriously, Napoleon reached Moscow by the middle of September. The retreating Russian army was shaken and scarred but by no means fatally undermined. It kept fighting occasionally or shadowing the flanks of the French army.

As the shrinking Grand Army entered Moscow, Napoleon found the city half deserted and stripped of provisions, and shortly afterwards devastating fires added to his miseries. The winter months were nearing and severe cold now threatened the poorly prepared army with disaster. After some hesitancy it was reluctantly acknowledged that there was nothing else to do but return westward. Thus began the ill-famed retreat from Moscow. By the time the self-defeated army reached the Russian border, after being harassed by guerrilla bands and tantalized by hunger and cold, it represented a demoralized aggregation of survivors hardly a sixth of its original size. By the end of 1812 Russian soil was entirely cleared of the invading French army, and the crucial question presented itself: "What next?"

**Russia and Europe.** The vital decision to be made by Alexander at this point was whether to conclude a favorable peace with Napoleon or drive farther west and free the continent of Bonapartism. After some hesitance and conflicting counsel Alexander took the latter step and in January, 1813, embarked upon a new phase of the war: from a patriotic war of liberation the conflict turned into a European war in which Russia was destined to play a paramount part. By the middle of March, Prussia had joined Russia as an ally and declared war against France; in August, Austria and Sweden joined the European Coalition, while England pledged financial aid to each member. The imposing allied armies crossed the French frontiers in 1814. Simultaneously, in accordance with the Treaty of Chaumont of March 1, 1814, each of the Allies pledged not to deal with Napoleon separately, but to fight until France was confined to her former borders, and then discuss a final peace settlement. On March 31 allied troops triumphantly entered Paris, spelling the end of the French Empire. On April 11 Napoleon abdicated and was sent off to Elba while Alexander reached the zenith of his career.

**The Search for Peace.** The immediate problem was a peace settlement, in which Russia's concern was the demarcation of her western border, involving mainly the solution of the Polish question. It was only after some prolonged diplomatic haggling that Alexander reluctantly yielded to a decision whereby Poland was to be divided once more. Prussia was granted the western part and Russia received the eastern part of the Duchy of Warsaw. Alexander declared the newly acquired territory a kingdom, to which he granted a constitution. The western border of Russia, as defined at the Congress of Vienna, remained virtually unaltered until the First World War.

The escape of Napoleon from Elba, followed by the "Hundred Days," let to the formation of a "European Concert" signed on November 20, 1815, with the purpose of guarding the continent against any future revolutionary changes. In this manner came the Quadruple Alliance, led by Metternich and aided by Alexander I, to serve as the champion of legitimism. The irony of the situation is obvious: the tsar who originally cherished constitutional schemes, and hoped to retire afterwards to private life, now assumed the role of hereditary monarchist and champion of European legitimacy. Henceforth he joined Metternich in frowning more and more upon all progressive ideas and libertarian principles. It was on the initiative of Alexander I that the Holy Alliance was conceived with the intention of ruling the continent of "Christian nations" on the principles of Christian charity and justice.

The Alliance, which Castlereagh referred to as "a piece of sublime mysticism" and Metternich regarded as a hollow sound, nonetheless was employed by the Austrian statesman as a convenient political weapon against any opponents of the recently established order.

**Postwar Domestic Affairs: Serfdom.** Domestic affairs were gradually beset by difficulties. The price of victory proved costly: the invaded areas were left devastated, the entire country was in a state of economic exhaustion, and inflation threatened the land with financial disaster. Some of the earlier reforms, such as those in the field of education, now came to a standstill or retrogressed. Industrial development was handicapped by the abandonment of protective tariffs in 1816, as pledged at Vienna, and above all by the institution of serfdom. Forced by war conditions, the government often supplied factories with serf labor and purchased most of the commodities produced. For the same reason the government largely determined the type of articles which the factories turned out. With the end of the war, production was bound to be drastically reduced. Furthermore, the enterprises that survived the post-war depression entered into sharp competition with those industries operating with free labor. The contest was instructive: the latter proved more efficient and dependable than those operated with serf labor. It indicated rather convincingly the harmful effects serfdom was bound to have upon industrial development in the nation. From the start of his reign Alexander I manifested a keen interest in the problem of serfdom but he was never able to cope with it successfully. In later years it was a source of profound melancholy to him to observe how little had been achieved since his ascendancy.

**Lessons in Emancipation.** After the war Alexander freed the serfs in the Baltic provinces during the years 1816, 1818, and 1819. This action demonstrated what was to be avoided in the future rather than repeated: since the serfs were emancipated without land they were bound to become economic slaves, even though legally free. The new problems at times outweighed the old ones. War and post-war experiences left a deep imprint upon Alexander's character and he became exceedingly cautious, fearful of coping with any of the issues or of

touching institutions that were corroding the social order.
He refused to promulgate legislation that might imply
compulsion, rash action, or hardship to the landed gentry.
Such an attitude was bound to stalemate rather than
solve problems emanating from the malignant institution
of serfdom.

**Rising Political Discontent.** Russia's participation in
the war awakened an enormous interest in public affairs
and kept alive hope that with the establishment of peace
Alexander would renew his effort to bring about political
reforms. The facts that Alexander granted Finland the
status of a Grand Duchy, that he gave Poland a constitution, and that he publicly planned to extend representative government to other parts of the Empire, seemed to
justify the anticipation of reforms. Furthermore, Alexander championed various free institutions in the west;
under his influence the restored Bourbons in France were
compelled to rule in accordance with a constitutional
charter. In 1818 Alexander once again demonstrated some
interest in a possible revival of constitutional projects,
but it came to nought. As he grew older he believed
more strongly than ever that sovereigns must never yield
to pressure and that any changes should be initiated by
lawful authorities. Europe had had enough of the turmoil
which led to Bonapartist tyranny. His views conflicted,
of course, with those held by the younger generation and
veterans of the recent war against Napoleon.

As the years went by, Alexander's philosophy came to
resemble that of Metternich. In 1820 the Semenovsky
Regiment of the Guards rose against what it considered
unjust treatment and unnecessarily rigorous discipline.
To Alexander it signified that even Russia was not immune to the western malady of revolution. His suspicion
was further confirmed by reports of the existence in
Russia of a clandestine society that sought political and
social changes. Members of this society were still in the
process of forming an organization crystallizing their
program and seeking means of attaining their goals, when
suddenly news came that on December 1, 1825, Alexander I had died in southern Russia.

There followed a brief interregnum, accompanied by
confusion, which ended with the ascendancy of Nicholas
I, who symbolized reaction. The prospect of a reactionary

tsar provoked a brief but ominous uprising, better known
as the Decembrist revolt, which colored the entire reign
of the new sovereign: he developed an exaggerated fear
of revolution which led him to the suppression of every
form of free thought in the country. Russia now fell
completely under the spell of another western malady—
Metternichism.

— 9 —

# THE REIGN OF NICHOLAS I,
## 1825-55

**Question of Succession.** It is important to bear in
mind the events that accompanied the ascendancy of
Nicholas I since these conditioned his philosophy for the
rest of his life. According to the Law of Succession of
April, 1797, the crown had to pass from father to the
eldest son. Since Alexander was childless, his successor,
therefore, had to be his brother Constantine, and since
Constantine had contracted a morganatic marriage he
had to renounce his claim in favor of his younger brother
Nicholas. It was never entirely clear that either Constantine or Nicholas had been duly informed of the
Manifesto naming the latter successor to the throne.
Neither one claimed to know of the existence of such a
document. Secret copies of the Manifesto were filed in
1822 with the Senate, the Synod, the Council of State,
and the Office of the Metropolitan of St. Petersburg.
When the news of Alexander's death was announced,
Constantine took the loyalty oath to his brother Nicholas
in Warsaw, where he resided, while Nicholas pledged his
loyalty to Constantine in St. Petersburg. For some three
weeks couriers kept running back and forth between the
two capitals in an effort to settle the matter. (*See Reading No. 11.*)

**The Decembrist Revolt.** Meanwhile, the members of a secret society dating back to 1816 hurriedly decided to take advantage of the temporary confusion. Under the slogan "Constantine and Constitution," they succeeded in stirring up several military units, who appeared on the Senate Square demanding that Constantine be placed on the throne. From the very start, what came to be known as the Decembrist revolt had little chance to succeed, though this pioneering effort was the prelude to the nineteenth-century Russian revolutionary movement. After some indecisive action, with attempts to persuade the rebels to return to their barracks peacefully, Nicholas crushed the revolt by force. Hundreds of its leaders and participants were imprisoned or exiled and five of the main instigators were hanged. The important feature to note is the profound impression the Decembrist revolt produced upon Nicholas: throughout his thirty-year reign he continued to suspect every public expression as nothing less than a revolt against legitimate authority.

**Personality of Nicholas I.** Nicholas I was born shortly before the death of his grandmother Catherine I; when he was five years old his father was assassinated in the notorious court plot. He, unlike his elder brother, was thus spared the fate of having to witness a jealous father barred from the household of an oversolicitous grandmother. Nicholas was brought up by his mother; his elder brother Alexander never interfered with his training. Like Alexander, Nicholas was tutored by a Frenchman. Unlike Laharpe who had taught Alexander I, this tutor was an emigré who loathed the French Republic, Republicanism, the Revolution, and everything associated with them. He imbued his pupil with an absolutist philosophy which remained unshaken during Nicholas' lifetime. The marriage of Nicholas to the daughter of Frederick William of Prussia in 1817 added little to his possible conversion to liberalism. After an extensive journey in western Europe Nicholas returned home with a deep sense of revulsion against any form of limited monarchy. He looked upon constitutionalism as the cause of both political corrosion and the decline of western civilization.

Since Nicholas was not considered for the throne until very late, his training was largely military, under the supervision of General Lamsdorff. He greatly admired military parades, and was noted for daily drills for the sole purpose of parading on the square of the capital. Nicholas took part in the campaigns of 1814-15, although he was not in combat. He did take part enthusiastically in victory parades in France and in the various German states. Later, as Inspector-General of the engineer corps, as Commander of the Guards brigade, and as Head of the Guards Division, he had discipline rigorously enforced and called for all the code required from the soldier of those days. Nicholas himself remained a soldier to the core all his life, despite his bearing of the crown. Whether it was the color or style of uniform, the type of ammunition, or the weight of arms to be carried by the individual sldier, all these were subjects of much greater concern to Nicholas than the plight of the peasantry.

From his early years Nicholas demonstrated qualities of obduracy and ill temper; he was quickly angered and easily hurt, he seldom acknowledged his own faults, and though normally timid, at times he displayed a certain bravado. His attempts to enforce rigorous military discipline led to serious grumbling among the soldiers. Unsociable, cold, inflexible, and severe, he was admired by few and feared by all. His candid manner bordered quite often on boorishness.

**Political Philosophy of Nicholas I.** Already in 1819 Alexander had spoken to Nicholas, informing him of his becoming successor. On December 26, 1825, Nicholas, twenty-nine years of age, mounted the throne. In a characteristically arrogant, self-assured way he plunged into action. His philosophy of government, his concept of what constituted social stability, is often compared with that of a sergeant. Absolutism he regarded as never to be questioned for a moment. A monarch, according to Nicholas I, was given divine rights to rule a country without interference. This to Nicholas was an absolute faith, an infallible truth which he held all his life to be incontestable.

Having assumed power, Nicholas I demanded absolute subordination to the throne. Under such a system the men who served the state had to submit to the royal will and were noted for their servility. With the exception

of a few (very few) stronger personalities in his minis-
tries, most of those who held official posts were pallid
figures; they were noted for neither initiative nor original
thought, being mere flunkeys willing to submit to the
Procrustean regime established under Nicholas. Since
Nicholas did not trust the various institutions he superimposed upon all of them a Private Chancellory, which
included the ill-famed "Divisions." One of these was the
notorious "Third Division," or Intelligence Department.
Over all these old and newly set up agencies reigned, of
course, the Autocrat of All Russias, Nicholas I. According to Nicholas, a state that tolerated free discussion,
that granted the right to question decrees from above,
invited chaos. Nicholas was entirely incapable of tolerat-
ing delegation of authority not strictly watched by the
vigilant eye of the sovereign. For this reason his reign
is noted for the increased bureaucratization and central-
ization of the entire administration. The reign of Nicholas
marks a period of so-called "secret-committees" that kept
discussing issues endlessly and fruitlessly, consuming tons
of paper, with results so meager that they tested even the
patience of Nicholas himself.

Blind self-confidence and denial of free initiative characterized the three decades of this reign. Anyone suspected of violation of the absolutists principle would
never be forgiven or forgotten. Always on his mind were
the Decembrists, to whom he frequently referred wryly
as *Mes amis du quatorze.* The strangest thing about Nicholas was that even though he was severe and heartless
with his subjects, he was gentle, kind, almost sentimental
with members of his family. That Nicholas loved his
country has never been denied, but he loved it as a sergeant loves his trusted company. It was a kind of love
in which the nation nearly stifled, the embrace of a bear
that threatens to crush one's ribs. The Crimean fiasco
was an appropriate climax to the regime that Nicholas I
had established in 1825.

**Domestic Affairs.** One of the problems was the constantly worsening issue of serfdom and the general state
of agriculture. The serf population increased while agricultural conditions remained medieval: both peasantry
and gentry felt the oncoming crisis. Serf labor became
unprofitable, yet the gentry were reluctant to free their

serfs or to give up their land without adequate compensation. On the other hand, the government looked askance at compulsion of any kind and continued to believe that its part must be entirely that of an honest broker between the negotiating parties. This led eventually to a total impasse typical of the later period of Nicholas' reign. General economic conditions in the country aggravated matters further. The preceding wars left behind them the usual lamentable legacy of valueless paper currency. It took nearly fifteen years of great effort before the silver ruble with a fixed value was established as the currency unit. But the wars with Turkey and Persia and the campaign of 1830 in Poland where suppression of the revolt came high, all served to undermine the constructive work of the able Minister of Finance, Yegor Kankrin. (1823-44).

**Uvarov as Minister of Education.** The policy of Nicholas I was bound to have serious effects upon the country's cultural life. The man who championed the cause of the Emperor in this field was the Minister of Education, Count Sergei Uvarov (1833-49). His policy, which received the blessing of Nicholas I, was to bend education toward a single goal—to train law-abiding subjects and perpetuate the social order. The entire educational system was to rest upon three pillars—Orthodoxy, Autocracy, and Nationalism—which presumably would guard the populace against the intellectual plague that ravaged western society. To this end, the schools were reorganized, or rather, bureaucratized. The educational system was based on the principle of class structure, each pupil to be enlightened in accordance with his social origin. Institutions of higher learning were stripped of their former autonomy as well as their authority in the field of secondary education; the university curriculum stressed only politically harmless subjects and curbed, or eliminated entirely, subjects in the social sciences.

Strangely enough, despite the suppression of free thought and the absolute reign of the censor, the 'forties were noted for the creative critical activities that affected the entire course of social and literary development in Russia. It was during the 'thirties and 'forties that Western and Slavophile views were crystallized, and that revolutionary ideas assumed purpose. These decades produced some of Russia's distinguished national leaders in the fields of literature and political thought. After the alarming events of 1848 in the West, the Russian government strained further to eradicate liberal thought and suppress every organization suspected of subversive proclivities. One of these was the Petrashevsky circle, whose members, including Dostoevsky, received the death sentence, which was later commuted to exile. The iron-fisted policy of the government managed to paralyze intellectual life after 1848. This policy was felt even abroad, when in 1849 the Russian army marched into Hungary to suppress the revolution against the Habsburg monarchy. Bitter were the feelings of Nicholas a few years later when he discovered what he referred to as the shocking "Austrian ingratitude" during the Crimean war.

Poland. National minorities during the reign of Nicholas I did not fare too well either. The fate of Poland is perhaps the most outstanding example. Poland was granted a constitutional form of government by Alexander I, with a bicameral legislature that had control over the executive as well as the power to levy taxes. The constitution provided for individual freedom and established a Polish army independent of the Russian armed forces. The commander-in-chief of the Polish army was Constantine, who, incidentally, violated the constitutional charter on many occasions. The July 1830 revolution in France had quick repercussions in eastern Europe, notably in Poland. By November the country was in the throes of a nationwide revolution which proclaimed the country an independent republic. A sovereign Polish republic was the last thing Nicholas wished to see on the doorstep of Russia, and he dispatched a huge force to crush it. By September, 1831, Warsaw was finally seized, despite the revolutionary valor of the rebels and the popularity of their cause throughout the West. The defeat of the short-lived republic ended the constitutional government that had functioned precariously since 1816. The charter which Alexander granted to Poland was now revoked; the independence of the Polish army was ended; and the use of the Polish language was prohibited. The freedom that had existed under national autonomy vanished rapidly, and the country thenceforth became part of the imperial system of Russia.

**Foreign Issues.** Elsewhere the initial policy of Nicholas I met with greater success. Early in 1829 the war with Persia culminated with the Treaty of Turkmanchai, according to which Russia won complete freedom of navigation in the Caspian Sea and gained the khanates of Erivan and Nakhichevan, thereby consolidating her position in the Caucasus. Even greater gains seemed to have been made at the expense of Turkey. In accordance with the Treaty of Akkerman of October 7, 1826, the provisions of the Treaty of Bucharest were reaffirmed, allowing passage of Russian ships in the Black Sea and in the Straits. The Treaty of Adrianople, signed on September 14, 1829, stipulated that ships of all nations were to be granted free passage through the Straits and that Russian merchants were to have unrestricted freedom to trade in Turkey.

**The "Eastern Question."** In the Near East, Russia encountered strong opposition from Austria and Great Britain. With Austria relations improved due to the fact that temporarily the two states were forced by a binding interest to defend monarchical interests in Europe. Had the Polish revolt of 1830 not taken place, the relationship might have been quite different, but absolutism and common interests in Poland brought Austria, Russia, and Prussia closer together. In the case of Great Britain the situation was different: the British government consistently opposed Russian penetration into the Mediterranean. Nicholas I believed that in the interest of Russia, at least in the foreseable future, the preservation of a weak Turkey would be preferable to the complete breakup of the Ottoman Empire, which was bound to end with the creation of several smaller Christian states in the Balkans. A weak Turkey would permit Russian intervention in Turkish affairs assertedly on behalf of the oppressed Christian minorities. Needless to say, neither Austria nor Great Britain shared this view.

**"The Sick Man of Europe."** In western Europe, Great Britain, supported by France, opposed Russia's assumed right of protectorship over Turkey or, in the case of France, her assertion of stewardship over the Christians in the Holy Places. For these reasons both western powers insisted that the Sultan should at all costs avoid internal conflicts, such as in case of Mehemet Ali in Egypt, which would serve to strengthen the position of Russia. Clashing opinions led, in February and April of 1833, to the sudden arrival of Russian land and naval forces at Constantinople and shortly afterwards at the Bosphorus. Though they left the same summer, prior to their departure they made the Sultan sign the Unkiar Skelessi Treaty on July 8, 1833. In accordance with this treaty Turkey, at Russia's request, might close the Dardanelles to warships of certain foreign powers. In October this stipulation was fortified further when Austria, Russia, and Prussia agreed that it was the perfect right of one sovereign state to call upon the aid of another in case of external or internal need. The implication of this agreement was self-explanatory as far as Russo-Turkish relations were concerned.

**Russia and England.** Although diplomatic developments in the early 'thirties were characterized by serious Anglo-Russian feuding over the Near Eastern Question, Nicholas I did not accept the threatening differences as entirely irreconcilable in nature; he exerted much effort to bring about a rapprochement with Great Britain. In May, 1839, Nicholas sent the Grand Duke and heir apparent Alexander on a good-will mission to England. He carefully let London know that if treaty obligations compelled Russia to render aid to Turkey he would act exclusively as representative of the western powers. Furthermore, Nicholas was willing to accept the closing of the Straits to all warships. If Great Britain and Russia, concluded Nicholas, could agree on these points then the Treaty of Unkiar Skelessi, which was to expire in 1841, need not be renewed. It seemed at this moment that Russia held the advantage, yet the course of forthcoming events did not culminate in the favorable outcome that had been anticipated with such assurance in St. Petersburg. When the old Sultan died at the end of June, 1839, and Mehemet Ali in Egypt was on the verge of a complete triumph, the western powers stepped in with an offer to mediate. The July mediations rendered Britain a diplomatic victory: Egypt was to become the hereditary possession of Mehemet Ali and, more important, the Powers undertook, by the Convention of 1841, to guarantee the neutrality of the Straits. This deprived Russia of her claim to exclusive rights as champion of Turkey's interests under the Treaty of Unkiar Skelessi.

**Nicholas and the Revolution of 1848.** The Convention of 1841 did not discourage Nicholas from seeking further means of agreement with Great Britain. In 1844 he paid a personal visit to London during which he endeavored to bridge the gap between the two countries by offering a mutually satisfactory plan for the "sick man of Europe." In case of the collapse of the Turkish Empire, Nicholas I hoped the two countries might act together to prevent a scramble for spoils in the Near East. But the British government remained cool toward the idea, and Nicholas turned for diplomatic support to other nations. To strengthen his position he sought further improvement in relations with Prussia and particularly with Austria. Thus, in 1846, when Austria —under the pretext of eradicating the seat of radicalism —occupied Cracow, the last remnant of what had been Poland, Nicholas raised no objection. In March, 1849, when the revolutionary tide of the preceding year had swept through Europe and was threatening Austria with political disintegration, the young Emperor, Francis Joseph, appealed for Russian aid, which Nicholas unhesitatingly granted. His readiness can be explained partly by the fact that he had a special dislike of the rebellious Hungarians who oppressed the Slavs, and partly because they threatened to inflame Poland. In May, 1849, the Russian army marched into Hungary and crushed the revolt. Nicholas calculated that not only was his country instrumental in forestalling revolution in eastern Europe, but by acting speedily he won the gratitude of an Austrian sovereign upon whom Russia could rely in the future.

Although Nicholas never let the Near Eastern Question lie dormant, the revolutionary events of 1848 kept Russia occupied in the West. During that year a Russian force, under the pretext of combating revolutionary activities, occupied the Danubian principalities. Under pressure from Great Britain and France, however, Nicholas was soon compelled to recall it. In 1849, when some of the revolutionary leaders fled to Turkey, both Austria and Russia demanded their extradition; the Sultan, supported by Great Britain and France, refused to comply. Though rebuffed on various occasions, Nicholas strangely enough was not disheartened, since he counted on Prussian cordiality and Austrian "gratitude"; he still hoped to alienate France from Great Britain and eventually come to an understanding with the British government.

**On the Eve of Conflict.** The Near Eastern crisis in 1851, however, emanated from the conflicting policies of France and Russia over matters that seemed irrelevant to the diplomatic issues at stake. For one thing, the Greek Orthodox and Roman Catholic churches were quarreling over custody of the Holy Place at Jerusalem. Nicholas I and Louis Napoleon, both motivated by other than religious reasons, decided to back the protectorship and special privileges of the respective churches. The Sultan, torn between the two, made concessions first to one side and then to the other, thereby antagonizing both. Russia demanded her rights as provided by the Kuchuk Kainardji Treaty, but the Sultan, backed by Great Britain and France, stood firm on a policy of his own choice. In July, 1853, Nicholas lost patience, occupied Moldavia and Wallachia, and declared that these provinces would be held until a satisfactory settlement was reached. Immediately French and British naval forces were ordered to the Dardanelles, despite Nicholas' last minute pleas to the British ambassador at St. Petersburg to find an amicable means for the partition of Turkey. Meanwhile, encouraged by the West's firm stand against Russia, Turkey sent an ultimatum on October 10, demanding the withdrawal of Russian troops from the occupied provinces; when the demand was not answered, Turkey declared war.

It was at this point that Nicholas I, who had high hopes that Austria would remain at least benevolently neutral, received the shock of "Habsburg ingratitude." In the midst of the crisis Austria and Prussia, after signing a defensive agreement presented Russia with a virtual ultimatum to evacuate Moldavia and Wallachia. The challenge could not be met. With a heavy and bitter heart Nicholas I could do nothing but bow to the demand. Momentarily it seemed as if further military action would be unwarranted. But instead the Allies decided to terminate Russian encroachment upon Turkey once and for all by proceeding with the originally planned campaign. The Crimean Peninsula was chosen as the most convenient ground for battle.

**The Crimean War.** After successfully landing at Eupatoria, the Allies advanced toward Sevastopol, where the famous siege took place. Russia's position was made especially difficult by Austria, which forced Russia to keep troops in the west while simultaneously fighting in the south. The siege of Sevastopol lasted precisely 350 days, and when on September 9, 1855, defeat was finally admitted, the Allies captured an entirely ruined city. The fall of Sevastopol served as a sobering blow to Russia: it awakened her to the realization that she was defeated there largely because of her own backwardness. Nicholas I did not live long enough to witness the end of the humiliating war, nor the crumbling of the social order he had so valorously championed. He died on March 2, 1855; the Treaty of Paris was signed on March 30, 1856.

**The Treaty of Paris.** According to the provisions of the Treaty of Paris, Russia was given back Sevastopol in return for Kars gained in the Caucasus; she had to cede southern Bessarabia to Moldavia, thereby barring her from the mouth of the Danube. Furthermore, the Black Sea henceforth was to be neutralized, and the Convention of 1841, which barred all warships from the Straits, was reaffirmed. Russia had to abrogate her former claims to protect Orthodox Christians within the Turkish Empire, and was thereby deprived of any future pretexts for intervention into Ottoman affairs. Finally, Turkey was henceforth to be permitted to participate in "public law and concert of Europe"; the European powers collectively agreed to guarantee "the independence and the territorial integrity of the Ottoman Empire."

# THE REIGN OF ALEXANDER II, 1855-81

**On the Eve of Reforms.** The Crimean defeat came as a rude awakening to the lamentable state of Russian affairs. The popular feeling was that the country was in dire need of change, including the removal of obsolete institutions. It was no wonder that following the death of Nicholas I questions of such reforms became an outburst throughout the country. Simultaneously, the cry went up for legislative freedom of discussion. The focal issue, however, remained the question of serfdom. There were enough opinions expressed as to how the problem could be effectively handled, but one general conviction united all; namely, that the Crimean war had closed a chapter of history and that a new era was beginning.

**The Personality of Alexander II.** The eldest son and successor of Nicholas I was Alexander II, born in Moscow in April 1818. Though destined to go down in history as the Tsar Emancipator during an "Era of Great Reforms," Alexander was a reformer neither by training nor by nature. The changes he was to introduce were motivated more by a desperate effort to forestall radical alterations than by a sense of historical necessity. As heir apparent, Alexander had been trained to bear the crown by preserving absolutism; he was to defend the rights of the gentry as the pillar of the monarchy. This, of course, implied the preservation of the appropriate institutions, including serfdom. Alexander II grew up, under the influence of his father, to consider autocracy a divine trust, the only form of government that made sense, and class structure as the most natural social organization that provided public order.

The early education of Alexander was guided by a certain Captain Merder, to be followed two years later by

V. A. Zhukovsky, the well-known Russian poet. The choice of Zhukovsky is interesting. Sensing that military indoctrination alone was not enough, Zhukovsky wrote a personal letter to the Empress, begging her to improve the education of her son and heir apparent. "Passion for military occupation will narrow his soul," contended Zhukovsky. "He will be accustomed to see in the people only a regiment, in his fatherland only the barracks." The future sovereign, Zhukovsky argued further, must not only be a general but a law-giver as well; in him must be cultivated a genuine sense of the people's need, for laws, for enlightenment, for a high level of moral upbringing. But Alexander's father could not understand the poet's thesis and insisted that without military science no sovereign could successfully rule a country. For this reason he felt that it should be given pre-eminence at the expense of all other subjects. Zhukovsky also expressed his profound regret that Alexander had travelled abroad extensively (mainly to Prussia) 1829-33, the crucial years when his attention should have been centered on his studies. Only once, in 1837, did Alexander tour Russia—a hasty journey accompanied by Zhukovsky.

Ill health compelled Captain Merder to resign his position as tutor in 1833; a few years later Zhukovsky's assignment also came to an end. Casual tutoring, frequently interrupted for one reason or another, continued until 1837. For about six months Speransky lectured to Alexander on the laws of the Empire. In 1838 Alexander was assigned to study advanced subjects in the military, financial, and diplomatic sciences. In each field his tutors were the corresponding ministers, Jomini, Kankrin, and Brunnow. By the end of 1838 the official education of Alexander had ended. According to Zhukovsky, Alexander had a lively and receptive mind, but he lacked persistence. This observation coincides with the view of his former tutor, Captain Merder. Later associates of Alexander recorded other observations, such as his arrogance, his extreme reluctance to concede that an opponent might be right, and his readiness to argue even in the face of obvious doubts of his own position.

As Alexander actively entered political life, he had to reject some of the beliefs so carefully implanted during his father's reign. Life posed new problems and forced him to seek new methods to solve them. Alexander faced these tasks cautiously, as if timidly feeling his way before undertaking anything that implied fundamental change. Although he was a thoroughgoing absolutist, Alexander nevertheless sensed that the old forms of life—the antiquated institutions so carefully guarded, the entire social structure so revered—had collapsed beyond hope of repair or maintenance. He could not fail to observe the sorrowful legacy left by the recent Crimean war; he witnessed the crumbling of the institution of serfdom, which his father had desperately endeavored to defend; and he could not help but notice the fatal weaknesses the old order had demonstrated during the years prior to his ascendancy.

**Domestic Issues.** The immediate issue faced by Alexander II was the conclusion of peace; only then could he give his attention to domestic affairs. Still, even while the government was preoccupied with the drafting of the peace treaty, there were adequate signs that the reign of the new sovereign held out promise of a departure from the old ways. Many of the recent oppressive restrictions —the ban on foreign travel, the gagging of the press, the harsh censorship, the rigid entrance requirements to the universities—were relaxed or removed shortly after the death of Nicholas I. The first definite signs of anticipated reform came in March, 1856, when Alexander II warned that it would be "better to commence abolition of serfdom from above than allow it to abolish itself from below." He therefore suggested that the gentry might give serious consideration to the problem.

**Government Takes Action.** Months went by, yet the nationwide discussions of serfdom bore no fruit. The passivity of the gentry was largely caused by a paralyzing disagreement resulting from the differences in local conditions. Where the soil was rich and productive, and serf labor consequently less profitable, the gentry was willing to grant the serfs freedom, though not land. Where, on the other hand, the land was poor, as in the north, and where the serfs were exploited either on the land or in industry, the gentry was willing to free the serfs and part with its land provided it was sufficiently remunerated. As a matter of fact, many landlords considered this a rare opportunity of ridding themselves of unproductive land at an attractive price. And so it became increasingly clear that the government not only would be forced to intervene but would have to employ compulsory measures to enforce emancipation. Other problems included the amount of land to be alienated, the methods of its evaluation, the means of payment, and its collection from the freed serfs. Finally, on March 3, 1861, the government took the momentous first step of issuing a Manifesto in which it declared that serfdom had been abolished.

**Abolition of Serfdom.** The Manifesto constituted a legislative act of enormous historic magnitude. It was a bold stroke at the old order, even though belated. Yet it carried with it so many signs of compromise and retreat that eventually it gave rise to a number of problems that were destined to harass the Empire for decades to come. The authorities wanted emancipation of the serfs with a minimum loss to the gentry; consequently the peasant gained his legal freedom but not his economic independence. Instead of being bound, as formerly, to the land, he was now tied to the commune by means of tax payments, periodic land redistribution, or his inability to obtain a passport in case of temporary departure.

Though the freed serfs were given land which theoretically could not be taken away from them, they did not, in a strict sense, own that land; it was paid for by the government, which was in turn reimbursed by the peasantry over a period of forty-nine years, at a specified annual amount known as the "redemption payments." The evaluation of the land was also not without interest: the government paid the landlords an amount equivalent to the benefit they would have derived from it had they utilized it during a period of a little under seventeen years.

There was no common yardstick for the entire country as far as the size of the individual allotments were concerned. This depended either upon local conditions or upon the quality of the soil. Whatever the size might have been, in no circumstances was it adequate and never did the allotted plots exceed those which the serfs had tilled prior to March, 1861. At best the individual lot would keep the peasant occupied for not more than three days per week, while the rest of the time he would have to seek employment from his former master. He would be compelled to earn money not only to keep body and soul together, but also to pay his taxes, his redemption payments, and other expenses which the new money economy had forced upon him. And the peasant population kept increasing while the amount of land remained the same, or decreased.

The abolition of serfdom marked the collapse of the entire medieval order of society. There followed a quest for many changes and the emergence of new institutions, one of which was the reorganization of local government. On January 13, 1864, a law was passed establishing a "Zemstvo," or local government. Accordingly, each district was authorized to set up its own assembly. Since the law was passed three years after the Emancipation Proclamation, when the initial zeal for reform had begun to wear off, the elections were not as free as had been originally anticipated. The gentry feared democratically elected assemblies and therefore saw to it that electoral laws precluded local administrations from falling into the hands of politically unreliable elements. But the law stipulated that members of the district assemblies must represent three groups in accordance with their respective property qualifications. The peasantry voted indirectly, since each commune first chose "electors," who in turn formed the district body that elected a prescribed number of members to the assembly. The second group of voters were those who owned a certain amount of land, in different localities varying from a minimum of 550 to as high as 1100 acres. The third group represented the townsfolk: men engaged in trade or industry, or owners of real estate in the urban areas. The peasantry was thus always outvoted, though the gentry was never able to dominate the council either: the law stated that no group could be represented by a larger number than the other two groups combined.

The Zemstvos. The country was divided into some 360 districts, each of which was gradually authorized to set up its own zemstvo, or district assembly. Each assembly was headed by an executive board responsible to the general assembly, which met annually. The district assemblies in turn elected representatives to the provincial assembly and the latter named its own executive board. The zemstvos were in charge of a multitude of functions:

they sponsored advanced methods in agriculture, administered elementary schools, maintained roads, took charge of public health, managed many hospitals, sponsored life and fire insurance, and directed social welfare. The zemstvos had authority to levy taxes for local and prescribed uses and eventually managed to extend their activities to many other fields. From time to time they conflicted sharply with centralized authority, which came to regard the zemstvos as seats of subversive activities. This was no surprise, for the local assemblies were the sole institution which had any semblance of representative government.

Of all the reforms that followed the abolition of serfdom, the law of December 2, 1864, dealing with the judicial system, stood out next in importance. It was based on the long experience of western European states and introduced vital principles into the newly established courts—equality before the law, public hearings, and a system of modern prosecution and defense; it divorced the judicial branch from the administration, named qualified jurists as judges with adequate pay, and assured their tenure against any administrative whims. It introduced trial by jury, though made an exception in the case of government officials or political offenders.

**Educational Reforms.** At no previous time was the country so keenly aware of its need for educational improvement as after 1861. Almost immediately after the accession of Alexander II, entrance into universities was facilitated, resulting in an appreciable increase in enrollment, which in turn made for other complications. Since Russian students demonstrated an unusual interest in political affairs, the Ministry of Education, headed by an extreme conservative, Admiral Putyatin, issued an order forbidding student organizations. This provoked a wave of protests and student unrest that necessitated police and in some cases army action. Finally Putyatin was dismissed and Alexander II named a new minister, A. V. Golovnin, who undertook the task of drafting a new code for the universities.

A group of professors were sent to western Europe to study conditions in foreign universities and make appropriate recommendations. On June 30, 1863, they published the University Code, which restored the autonomy originally granted to universities in 1804. Official administrative interference was drastically reduced and the faculty was given authority to administer university affairs. On December 1, 1864, the Secondary Education Code established the Gymnasium and the Real School, one intended to prepare students for universities, the other for technical institutions of higher learning. The Elementary School Code, published on June 26, 1864, authorized municipal governments and zemstvos to found and maintain schools; their supervision was to be carried out by district school boards set up for that purpose.

As time went on and the ardor for change subsided further, the few reforms that followed bore the imprint of conservativism. Thus, when municipal government came up for reform in June, 1870, the law provided for a strict delineation of the tax-paying and non-paying voters: it divided the municipal electorate into three groups, according to the amount of taxes each paid. Municipal governments were authorized to levy taxes for their local needs, and to take charge of problems pertaining to education, public health, and similar needs. One serious handicap was that municipal authorities did not have any authority over the police, the latter being entirely within the jurisdiction of the central government.

**Army Reforms.** The last, though far from the least, of the reforms dealt with the army. The Crimean war swelled the armed forces by more than two million men, and still they were defeated by a much smaller allied force at Sevastopol. The reasons for this humiliating experience were not too difficult to find. In addition to the economic backwardness of the country, the huge distances and the archaic means of transportation paralyzed the military authorities. With the exception of a few distinguished officers, the army lacked leaders, and suffered from appalling administrative inefficiency, corruption, and an absence of coördinated effort; the medical branch was completely inadequate, and epidemics took a heavier toll than enemy fire.

Dimitri Miliutin, the newly appointed Minister of War and perhaps one of the most enlightened and able men in the government, set out to correct all these shortcomings. He did much to modernize the Russian army during his long term of office. The period of service was reduced, training for a military career was improved by setting up new and superior schools, technical equipment was brought up to date, the judiciary branch of the armed forces was reorganized, and punitive measures were humanized. In 1874, at the recommendation of Miliutin, the Military Service Law was passed. The new law imposed universal obligatory service for all young men twenty years of age. They were drafted for a period of six years, after which they were enlisted in the reserve militia for fourteen years. The entire country was divided into military districts, and each district was assigned annually a quota of young men to be chosen by lot. The same law also provided for an exemption or reduction of length of service, the former to be granted to family breadwinners or single sons, the latter depending upon the level of education reached by the men prior to enlistment.

**Discontent—Left and Right.** The Era of Great Reforms in Russia aroused many formerly dormant social forces which, once awakened, could hardly be suppressed. Many reforms were administered by the old bureaucracy, most of whom carried out their assigned tasks with little enthusiasm, with skepticism of the wisdom of adopted policies, or even with unconcealed animosity. Here were hidden the omens pointing toward a feud to come between officialdom, lacking faith in the reforms, and the liberal elements, who insisted upon the reforms as a logical sequence of the emancipation of the serfs. The gentry was largely conservative or sullen, and was apt to regard the course chosen by Alexander as fraught with grave social consequences. They looked upon any tampering with their age-old privileges as politically dangerous and maintained that unless their members were granted the right to more effective administrative control the government was toying with fate. Only a minority of the gentry believed that social upheaval could be forestalled by more definite guarantees of individual freedom, by a judicial branch free from administrative interference, by greater initiative in local government, and a responsible administration.

**The Intelligentsia.** The advocates of further administrative reforms came largely from the class commonly referred to as the intelligentsia—enlightened younger men and women who, because of freer access to universities had succeeded in obtaining an education. They were therefore able effectively to express their views orally or in the press on many vital issues of a social, economic, or political nature. It was from among the ranks of the intelligentsia that advocates of socialist ideas made their early appearance in the country. They went far ahead of the liberal gentry: whereas the latter merely recommended that the government summon a freely elected national assembly to consider further measures, the intelligentsia advocated immediate social reforms, elimination of social and economic inequality, and the granting of political freedom. Some went even further, rebelling against the institution of the family, the church, and the absolute monarchy. Such were the seeds soon to sprout into revolution in Russia.

To combat these subversive ideas the administration turned its attention to the press: it closed certain publications and prosecuted some of the writers or their editors. Among the latter was Chernyshevsky, who was exiled to Siberia. The Polish rebellion of 1863, provoked by a new conscription law, drove the government to further acts of suppression. After discovery that some of the radical elements sympathized with the Polish cause, the government leveled accusations of treason against the entire intelligentsia. In April, 1866, a flagrant attempt was made to assassinate Alexander II; the administration now decided to act quickly and with force. It evidently resolved to stamp out any sign of subversion even if it had to throw overboard some of the recently initiated reforms. The administration was so severe that progressive members of the cabinet handed in their resignations. This act only allowed the most conservative members of the gentry to seize the initiative in an effort to turn back the clock of history, with violent repercussions. The revolutionary movement was fast coming of age.

Among those who bore the brunt of reactionary policies were the schools. One of the measures introduced by the recently appointed Minister of Education, Tolstoy, changed the curriculum to a vacuous program that deadened intellectual aspiration. Science was looked upon as the source of nihilism—the philosophy that negated state, church, and family—and therefore, had to be curtailed.

The social sciences and even literature did not escape the ban. The new emphasis was upon classical languages, grammar, medieval Slavonic, mathematics, and similar subjects. Entrance into secondary schools became exceedingly difficult, and students who did manage to pass their examinations were subjected to such artificially created barriers that they did not last long. The universities could hardly escape the severity of the same policy, which caused considerable unrest among the students during the 'seventies.

**The Zemstvos Under Fire.** The zemstvos came to work under severe handicaps. Despite all the artificially created difficulties, the zemstvos made surprising progress in the field of elementary education. Handicapped financially, they nevertheless managed to build and operate schools in many parts of the country. Many of their difficulties arose from the fact that not only was their power to levy taxes limited, but in the late sixties their administrative authority had also been curbed. To a large extent their progress was due to a small but active group of intellectuals and liberal gentry who devoted all their talent and energy to the cause of education. The central authorities subjected zemstvo officials to various kinds of disheartening control: discussions were restricted to "subjects within their competence" and the administration defined competence in a very narrow sense; zemstvo proceedings were strictly censored before publication and often banned altogether; even the right to assemble was at times curbed. It is no wonder that the zemstvos in the 'seventies became acrimoniously critical of administrative policy, and that the administration in its turn saw the zemstvos as seats of subversion.

Emboldened by the authorities' fear of revolutionary terrorism, the elements that had been tacitly opposing reforms now launched vigorous attacks against all innovations introduced since 1861. One of these particularly under criticism was the jury system. Nor were the reactionaries enamoured with the idea of an independent judiciary or with the seeming leniency of some of the judges themselves. Political trials were finally shifted from regular to police courts, thus by-passing the jury system as well as some of the "unreliable" judges. Fear of free discussion led to an outcry against the abuses of the free press. The period of comparative freedom enjoyed by the press following the death of Nicholas I proved short-lived. After 1866, when the police were authorized to try cases of violation by the press of its freedom, new rules began to gag all writing. Penalties for even minor infringements became so indiscriminate and severe that papers and magazines critical of government policy faced virtual closure. In this manner, of course, the opposition was successfully silenced.

**General Economic Conditions.** The Crimean experience manifested not only political deficiencies: in fiscal matters also a state of confusion prevailed. It was only after the war that the Minister of Finance assumed sole authority over national revenue and expenditure. Modern state budgeting, only introduced in 1862, aided considerably in placing the national economy on a sound basis. Although serfdom—one of the supreme barriers to amelioration of conditions—existed no longer, its sorrowful heritage was felt for years. There was a crying need for improvement in means of transportation and communication. The country lacked banking institutions to stimulate business, and private capital was entirely inadequate to cope with the needs of the nation. Economic backwardness called for huge outlays of capital, for long-range investments with no quick returns. Railroad construction, the founding of banking enterprises, and the setting up of industrial plants called for state aid and state participation. Some industrial enterprises soon faced critical labor shortages. In the iron and wool industries, which formerly employed serf labor, production dropped alarmingly. It took more than a decade for the country to recover from the effects of the Act of Emancipation. When, however, economic conditions at last seemed better, Russia had to taste the bitter fruit of the industrial economy—depression. It took almost another decade before the country was able to recover from the shock of the industrial crisis of 1878-79.

**External Affairs.** In the realm of foreign affairs, Russia was, after the Crimean war, in search of a new national orientation. Whereas prior to 1853 she had based her policy on coöperation with the other two monarchies, Prussia and Austria, the war proved to Russian statesmen that this was dangerous. The conduct of

Austria during the war was neither forgotten nor easily forgiven, and some new alignment had to be sought. At first it seemed as if France might be the country with which coöperation would be feasible. But the sympathetic view taken by the French government toward the Polish rebellion in 1863 ended further cultivation of Franco-Russian friendship. That left Prussia, with whom relations were traditionally cordial. These two countries, besides the fact that they were bound by a mutual need to protect monarchical institutions, were also tied by royal kinship, Alexander being the nephew of William I of Prussia (Nicholas I was married to the sister of William I). Another common bond was their need to maintain peace in Poland. For this reason Prussia rendered much aid to the Russian army during the Polish rebellion: it permitted Russian guards to pursue fleeing rebels into Prussian territory, while at the same time it guarded the frontiers against any Polish refugees who endeavored to escape to the West. Russia rendered similar assistance during the Austro-Prussian war in 1866, and particularly during the Franco-Prussian war of 1870, which Russia prevented Austria from joining. In return, Prussia consented to Russia's repudiation, in November, 1870, of the clause of the Treaty of Paris which stipulated the neutralization of the Black Sea. Following the Franco-Prussian war Bismarck continued to insist that German-Russian coöperation was the only course for the German Empire. The "Three Emperors' League," of September, 1872, aimed at the maintenance of peace on the continent, provided for common action in case of crisis in the Near East, and agreed to combat revolutionary activities. This cordiality, sometimes strenuously tested, nonetheless lasted as long as Bismarck remained in power. The most serious difficulty that taxed the friendship of the three monarchies was the chronic crisis in the Near East, where Austrian and Russian interests became incompatible.

**The Near East Again.** The Crimean War did not solve the Near Eastern riddle nor did it alleviate the sorrowful lot of Christian minorities in Turkey. The reforms solemnly pledged by the Sultan remained on paper, and the collective protection the Allies promised did not materialize: the only recourse left for the Christians was sporadic outbursts of violence against their oppressors.

One such outbreak took place in 1875 in Bosnia and Herzegovina and was immediately given support by Serbia and Montenegro. The uprising threatened to turn into a general Balkan revolt, the very thought of which made Austria shudder and Britain fearful of Russian penetration into the Near East. It was for this reason that Vienna sought all possible means to restore peace quickly and kept urging the Sultan to carry out the promised reforms. The oppressed minorities, however, after being deceived too long by false promises, had no more patience and refused to lay down their arms until they gained independence. When, finally, it became clear that a Russo-Turkish conflict seemed imminent, Austria consented to remain neutral provided she would be rewarded territorially at the end of such a war. After Russia had accepted this condition it was only a matter of time before the war began.

**Outbreak of War.** In July, 1876, Serbia and Montenegro declared war on Turkey, but after a few weeks of fighting Serbia faced a disastrous defeat unless Russia came to her aid. Despite the uncertain neutrality of Austria and the certain enmity of Britain, Russia declared war on Turkey on April 24, 1877. The Russian army was in the midst of reorganization in accordance with the military reforms introduced by Miliutin; for this reason the campaign was no triumphal march. Victories were gained only at the price of bloody fighting. It was not until January, 1878, that the Russian army entered Sofia, where the Turks were badly defeated. On the ninth of the same month Adrianople was seized and the Russians headed toward the Sea of Marmora; in the Caucasus Armenia had already fallen into Russian hands. The British became alarmed and began to prepare themselves for any contingency. On January 31, 1878, a Russian demarcation line was set up at Adrianople; shortly afterwards a British naval force sailed toward Constantinople to watch further moves. For a moment the war reached a critical phase and Austria suggested that a peaceful settlement be reached by means of an international congress rather than bilateral negotiation. The plan was accepted by all concerned, and it was agreed that the nations should meet at Berlin, where Bismarck accepted the part of "honest broker."

**From San Stefano to Berlin.** On March 3 Russia and Turkey signed the Treaty of San Stefano, which provided for the independence of Montenegro, Serbia, and Rumania, and established a "greater" Bulgaria which extended from the Black Sea to the Aegean, reaching out as far west as the Albanian mountains. This new Bulgarian state was to elect its own prince, a vassal of the Sultan, and be subject to approval by the European Powers. Russia also gained the regions of Kars, Batum, Ardahan, and Bayazid. Dobrudja was to be given to Rumania; in return she was to cede to Russia the part of Bessarabia that Russia had relinquished at Paris in 1856. The Treaty of San Stefano practically expelled Turkey from the continent of Europe. Neither Britain nor Austria agreed to accept this and requested that the Congress of Berlin re-examine the hastily drawn treaty. Russia yielded, though she calculated that at the anticipated congress she would be aided by Germany. But Gorchakov, the Russian Foreign Minister, had miscalculated his move: he discovered more "ingratitude" when Bismarck proved reluctant to act against both Austria and Great Britain. To her chagrin, Russia had no choice but to accept the alterations made by the Congress, after which the new treaty appeared very different. Bulgaria was considerably reduced and so were Serbia and Montenegro, while Bosnia and Herzegovina were to be occupied by Austria for thirty years. Rumania, Serbia, and Montenegro became independent states, and Rumania received part of Dobrudja in return for the strip of Bessarabia restored to Russia. Bayazid was to be given back to Turkey, and Batum was declared a free port. Such were the main revisions of the Congress of Berlin of July, 1878. The Near Eastern question assumed a new character in which Russia and Austria faced each other as rivals for control of the Balkans.

**Nihilism and Terrorism.** Nihilism marked the adolescence of the rebellious generation of Russia. There were many youths who looked askance at peaceful propaganda, who believed that it would lead nowhere unless the government was forced by intimidation to yield to the demands of the people. For this reason they advocated terror as the only weapon to advance their philosophy; they were responsible for the assassination of a number of high officials, including—eventually—the Tsar himself. The men formed a clandestine organization, "The Will of the People," which played a considerable part during the last quarter of the nineteenth century in Russia.

There were others who felt that perhaps the same goals might be attained by peaceful means. A purely negative philosophy, these believed, was not enough; freedom could not be won unless it was a constructive part of the sentiment of the masses. This sparked a movement "To the People": new ideas were to be propagated and the peasantry enlightened and made to realize that the cause of their plight was the social order—the only way to improve their lot was to rebel against tsarism. Neither philosophy proved entirely successful and only indicated the birth pangs of the revolutionary movement in the nineteenth century.

**Assassination of Alexander II.** Shortly before the death of Alexander II, a glimmer of hope appeared in the person of General Loris Melikov, Minister of the Interior, who hoped, with Alexander's encouragement to moderate the repressive policies by mild concessions. This could be achieved by summoning representative committees to render advice to the State Council. Some writers charitably called this the "Loris Melikov Constitutional Project." On the very day the decree was signed, the terrorists succeeded in their long-projected goal: while returning to his residence on March 13, 1881, Alexander II was killed by a bomb hurled at him by a member of one of the secret revolutionary organizations. It was ironic that Alexander II, who began his reign as "Liberator" of the serfs, should have been murdered by a member of an organization that called itself "The Will of the People." (*See Reading No. 12.*)

# — 11 —

# THE REIGN OF ALEXANDER III, 1881-94

**The Man and His Time.** The thirteen-year reign of Alexander III stands out in history as a last desperate effort to retain autocracy free from any democratic or constitutional impurities. The new ruler defended his cause like a knight in shining armor. Alexander III was the second son of Alexander II, born in 1845, when his father was still the Crown Prince. Together with his elder brother Nicholas, he was entrusted to a group of tutors headed by Lieutenant-General N. B. Zinoviev. The two brothers were as different as day and night. One was brilliant and quick, the other dull and slow, even though diligent. Among their tutors two must be especially noted: one was the eminent historian, S. M. Soloviev, the other the equally eminent reactionary staesman and spokesman for the monarchy, K. P. Pobedonostsev.

In the summer of 1864, Nicholas went abroad and for the first time left his brother Alexander all to himself. While abroad, Nicholas became engaged to the Danish princess Dagmar. Then a tragedy befell the family: on April 24, 1865, Nicholas died of tuberculosis. No one was more stricken by the sorrowful news than his younger brother Alexander, who shortly after the funeral was named successor to the throne. In November, 1866, Alexander married the former fiancée of his deceased brother, who became known afterwards as Maria Feodorovna. Since Alexander was not being originally groomed for the throne he had been brought up as a soldier, which meant that his training for royal responsibilities was woefully inadequate. (*See Reading No. 13.*)

During the last quarter of the century Alexander III faced overwhelming problems, which were totally alien and incomprehensible to him. Parochial of mind, stubborn, and temperamentally frigid, he seemed ill fitted to grasp the significance of the course of events before his eyes. As he observed a continuous rise of revolutionary activities and ideas in the country, he reached a simple conclusion: the widespread sedition was caused by the freedom which his father had granted the people and for which he had paid with his own life. Before his eyes the entire social structure had been caving in rapidly and surely. At the end he witnessed his father blown to bits by a revolutionary bomb. Small wonder that when he reached the throne Alexander was convinced that his ascendancy was providential, that he was sent by divine grace to save the Empire from the ravages of revolution. He seemed to have reached the throne with a single mission in mind—to combat subversion. There is a monument to this sovereign which survived the revolution—a gigantic statue of Alexander III mounted on a house, which in turn is mounted on a huge square block. The statue seems to convey the very spirit of the period: *status quo*. The equestrian and the horse stand frozen, as if determined to move neither forward nor backward: no political concessions, no limitations upon dynastic prerogatives.

**Reaction in Full Force.** In his Manifesto of May 11, 1881, Alexander III made his political philosophy quite clear. He professed absolute faith in autocracy as an infallible institution, which he had every intention of consolidating, preserving, and defending against any challenge. This caused even the most moderate members of the ministerial cabinet, including General Loris Melikov, to resign their posts. The new cabinet proceeded moderately at first, endeavored to aid the peasant, and sought a common ground upon which local and central authorities might reach some understanding. Within a year, however, there was a swing to the extreme right which did not waver until the end of the reign of Alexander III. In May, 1882, with the appointment of Count Dimitry Tolstoy, who replaced Count Ignatiev, reaction began in full force.

**Pobedonostsev—Voice of Autocracy.** The paradox was that the weaker the opposition became, the more reactionary grew the administration. The incarnation of this reactionary force was K. P. Pobedonostsev. A lawyer by training, one-time tutor of Alexander III (who felt Pobedonostsev's influence long after his ascendancy), member of the Loris Melikov Commission, and Head of the Holy Synod from 1889 to 1905, Pobedonostsev dominated the political scene from behind the Russian throne. He regarded all reforms as dangerous from their very inception, since any institution that arose therefrom was "systematically remade according to false principles." He was "disgusted" with what took place in the sixties and felt "as if he were living among children who fancy they are grown up." As tutor, he taught the Crown Prince that if a people have no unified authority or faith in their government, the inevitable consequence is chaos. As soon as Alexander III ascended the throne Pobedonostsev urged him "to end at once, now, all the talk about freedom of the press, about high-handed meetings, about a representative assembly."

**Damming the Tides of Time.** The protagonist of Russian autocracy, Pobedonostsev, became the idol of the rightist wing of the gentry. They followed their mentor in believing that all the reforms begun in 1861 were bound to lead to calamity; they saw only one solution, a revitalization of autocratic rule and the effective check upon the ideas that kept infiltrating into Russia. They felt that the entire idea of political freedom was fallacious, a sheer mirage, and that constitutional government could lead to nothing but administrative inefficiency, hollow loquacity, and narrow class selfishness. Freedom of the press under democratic rule was bound to end in license, sensationalism, corruption, factual distortion, deceit, and demagogy. Democratic justice resulted in casuistry and was essentially void of true legal justice.

According to the same school of political thought, the reforms were instrumental in destroying the valuable class structure of society; this in turn gave rise to the intelligentsia—that superfluous, variegated social group which had lost contact with the people as well as the state, and which represented an aimlessly drifting, constantly nagging, always restless element forever aiming at impractical, nonrealistic goals. The reaction of the rightists to the threat of the intelligentsia was just what one would expect: they refurbished the "articles of faith" of a bygone era—Orthodoxy, Autocracy, and Nationalism. They believed that society must be rejuvenated by restoring the class character which would permit the gentry once more to assume the leading position it had lost in recent years.

**Consolidation of the Regime.** Since this policy was aimed against the intelligentsia, the schools were the first to feel its impact. The new Code of 1884 extended the authority of the Minister of Education at the expense of the University Council. Student organizations were completely banned, and students suspected of violating new regulations were harshly dealt with. Secondary education was even more drastically altered: to complete a secondary education became a high privilege discreetly granted to few. The zemstvos under the new law of 1890 provided the conservative gentry with a majority able to dominate local administration. On the one hand, the peasantry was further restricted in its electoral rights; on the other, the gentry were henceforth appointed from a list of candidates compiled by the provincial governor. Local officials took over various zemstvo committees whose powers had been vastly extended. The former caste spirit of the officers' corps was restored. The judiciary, which had been the target of bitter criticism for some time, was stripped of its former independence. The peasant communes fell under the strict supervision of government-appointed officials. There was little in autocracy's battle about which to be jubilant, however, in view of the general economic and political state of the country.

**The Peasantry.** The peasantry was rapidly deteriorating, so in the summer of 1881 the government sought counsel from local officials. They urged extension of peasant allotments, reduction of redemption payments, and systematic, government-regulated eastward migration from congested areas in the west. The cause of the oncoming crisis was primarily the continuous growth of rural population without a proportionate increase in individual land holdings. Even the original grants were inadequate, while the periodic reapportionments resulted in further decrease of allotments. The peasants were in desperate need of capital: where the land was fertile and profitable to till, it was almost impossible to rent;

when it did happen to be available, it fell quickly into the hands of those who needed it less—speculators and kulak peasants. Individual migration was difficult since the cost was nearly prohibitive, and many peasants were tied to the commune anyway. Government aid was indispensable. Taxation became a crushing burden, while general rural conditions became so precarious that a single crop failure, it was justly feared, would spell national disaster. The Peasant Land Bank, established in 1881, proved of little value to the vast majority of the peasantry. In 1882 the government was compelled to reduce redemption payments and in 1883 to abolish the poll tax that had been in effect since the days of Peter I. This aided the peasants though it did not touch the real source of their plight. When a drought in 1891 ruined the entire crop in some twenty provinces it took the efforts of every conscientious subject to avert a national upheaval. But the experience also pointed up an intolerable state of affairs with which the administration proved incapable of coping.

**Urban Conditions.** The conditions of industrial workers was equally serious. The brief period of industrial expansion during the 'seventies had ended with a sudden crisis, and by 1880 the workers found themselves in the grip of an economic depression. It was the nation's earliest such experience, but it revealed the sorry lot of the urban workers. Low wages, followed by unemployment, inadequate housing, and lack of security, combined to create a formidable socio-economic crisis. The government had previously been warned of such a possible development but it refused to intervene in what it considered purely private business. The 1879-80 depression finally convinced the administration that official action was necessary, if for no other reason than fear of political repercussions. The law of 1882 was aimed at the termination of child labor and the limitation of working hours. The law of 1885 limited the ages of women and children employed on night shifts. The following year brought legislation concerning both employers' and workers' conditions of dismissal or leaving and the right of employees to monthly instead of annual pay, as was formerly the practice. One of the main demands of the workers, however—the right to form unions—was refused by the government; it outlawed both unions and strikes and declared any participation in either a criminal offense.

By the middle of the eighties the country had begun to recover from the first economic crisis. Protected by favorable tariffs, Russian industry could recover and advance. Capital at home was greatly augmented by foreign investments attracted by the recent sound financial policy of Witte, the adoption of the gold standard in 1897, and the government's contracting of loans abroad to finance industrial development at home. The result was that during the decade of 1887-97 the value of goods produced more than doubled; while the ranks of workers increased nearly seventy-five per cent. By the turn of the century Russia was face to face with an industrial revolution and all its ensuing consequences, the bitter taste of which the country sampled in 1899, when a second, a more severe crisis developed. By 1902 a large number of workers had lost their jobs, factories had closed down, prices were falling rapidly, and money had become scarce; yet the market was overstocked. The nation began to recover only in 1904, when the Russo-Japanese war broke out and combined with the recent economic crisis to pave the road to the forthcoming political unrest.

**Diplomacy Under Alexander III.** In the field of diplomacy equally important developments took place. The Congress of Berlin was a profound disappointment to Russia, for it proved beyond doubt her conflict of interests with Austria in the Balkans and increased her distrust in the value of coöperation with Germany. For this reason Alexander III's diplomacy underwent serious scrutiny leading to a cooling of relations with both countries. This led, at least in part, to closer Austro-German coöperation best manifested in the dual alliance concluded in October, 1879. Yet Bismarck feared, as did William I, that any alienation of Russia might lead that country toward friendlier relations with France—a development they would preclude at all cost. As long as she was at the helm, Germany pursued a policy of cordial relations with Russia. It was taxed at times by doubts of loyalty, and questioned on the degree to which Germany had supported Russia, but basically a pattern of cordiality was followed.

As, one by one, the earlier leaders of the German Empire were removed from the scene of national life, relations with Russia became more strained. At the time of Alexander II's death, Russo-German relations temporarily improved. In 1883 Foreign Minister Gorchakov, who deeply disliked Bismarck, resigned and shortly afterwards died. But Austro-Russian conflicts in the Balkans proved irreconcilable, and the new German coöperation with Austria alienated Russia still further.

During his last years in office Bismarck tried to prevent the imminent danger of a Franco-Russian alliance by concluding a highly secret three-year Russo-German agreement originally drawn up in 1884. It was a last desperate—and ultimately futile—attempt on the part of the Iron Chancellor to "reinsure" coöperation between Berlin and St. Petersburg and thereby keep Paris diplomatically isolated. Alexander III, much as he disliked the French Republic and its government, hated the Germans even more. The death of William I and the ascendancy of William II destroyed the slender royal tie between the two monarchies. Bismarck's resignation in the spring of 1890 completed the change of scene.

**The French Orientation.** What Bismarck feared most was now bound to occur: diplomatic isolation forced Russia to cultivate friendlier relations with France, who was only waiting for such an opportunity to break out of the ring forged around her by Bismarck. And Russia, realizing that it was too precarious to depend upon the Prince of Montenegro (as Alexander III tartly put it on one occasion) as her "only sincere and faithful friend," was ready to embrace even a Republican state as an ally. In this manner the two nations began to gravitate toward each other.

At first Franco-Russian relations improved through closer financial ties: Russia contracted French loans and placed ammunition orders. The two countries moved toward military negotiations in 1891, when a French squadron paid a courtesy visit to Kronstadt. The reception given the French turned into a huge diplomatic demonstration. Two years later the two countries concluded a commercial treaty and in the fall of the same year, 1893, the Russian fleet paid a return visit to Toulon. Already in 1892 a military convention had been drawn up; it was accompanied by a secret treaty of alliance and signed in March, 1894, as a countermove against the Austro-German Alliance. The course of events fearfully anticipated by Bismarck began to take recognizable shape in the later division of Europe into two diplomatic camps. Within two decades after Bismarck's death, however, the three monarchies—Germany, Russia, and Austria—had gone the way of all flesh.

— 12 —

# THE REIGN OF THE LAST ROMANOV, NICHOLAS II, 1894-1917

**Personality of Nicholas II.** Nicholas II ascended the throne with a single goal—preservation of autocracy. That was the bequest of his father; that was the ambition of his wife; that was his own desire. Yet few predecessors had come to power at a less favorable moment in history, nor was there a person less fit than Nicholas II for the task which he assigned himself. Alexander III, though exceedingly narrow-minded, was at least endowed with an iron will. Nicholas II, on the other hand, possessed a more ingratiating personality than his father, but he was an extraordinarily weak person with no clear purpose nor great vision. He was narrow intellectually and obdurate to the point of toying with fate, which was bound in the end to bring tragedy upon him, his family, and the nation.

In his early years he had a brief love affair with a well-known ballerina named Kseshinskaya, but his father opposed it and sent Nicholas on a long journey to cool off. In October, 1890, Nicholas journeyed through Vienna, Trieste, Greece, Egypt, India, China, and Japan, where he was attacked by a Japanese in the city of Otsu and narrowly escaped death. From Japan he went to Vladivostok, then across Siberia, and back to the capital which he reached in August, 1891, after travelling some nine months. In November, 1894, hardly a month after his father's death. Nicholas married Alexandra, formerly Princess Alix of Hesse-Darmstadt and granddaughter of Queen Victoria. She served to accentuate those very characteristics which contributed to the downfall of the monarchy. The tragic fact was that the Empress showed strength and stamina where weakness might have been a saving grace. Her pertinacious clinging to matters that history itself had foredoomed resulted in the tottering and eventually the crash of the Empire which she so vigorously tried to save.

**Warning Against "Senseless Dreams."** The early years of the reign of Nicholas II started portentously. On the occasion of his marriage various zemstvo representatives came to express their felicitations. Among them were representatives of the Tver province who were noted for their liberal proclivities, and who counseled the young sovereign that would be politically wise to heed the wishes of the people. Rather than give them at least an evasive reply, Nicholas II delived, at the suggestion of Pobedonostsev, a most tactless warning: he advised them not to be carried away by "senseless dreams" to expect greater freedom or more active participation of the zemstvos in the life of the nation than during the previous reign. (*See Reading No. 14.*) The Russo-Japanese war, followed by the social turmoil in 1905, compelled him to accept certain limitations upon the absolute monarchy, though with hidden reservations which in reality would nullify the concessions.

**General Conditions.** General conditions in the country at the time of the ascendancy of Nicholas II were far from encouraging. Many areas had hardly recovered from the devastating effects of the recent famine. Although the lot of some peasants had improved appreciably, the majority barely subsisted; there was a general land hunger while many of the peasants were on the verge of complete bankruptcy. Indebtedness became progressively worse, as arrears in redemption payments kept accumulating annually. The cost of manufactured goods was prohibitive to the peasants, for their earnings were exceedingly low. Eastward migration proved financially difficult, legally complicated, and therefore slow.

Despite the agrarian difficulties, industrial development kept making impressive progress. Foreign investments continually increased, notably in the coal, oil, and metallurgical industries. Side by side with the landed gentry arose a new class, the bourgeoisie, and the two were sheltered by the bureaucracy of the absolute monarchy headed by the Autocrat of All Russias. The reforms of the 'sixties and the 'seventies were followed by the emergence of a moderate liberal element usually associated with the local administration or the zemstvo. They were, in a good many cases, suspected of seditious ideas and zemstvo officials were often handicapped in their earnest efforts to bring about general economic and cultural improvement. Despite all impediments, the zemstvos managed to make impressive advancement in many fields—notably in public health, public education, and agriculture.

**Political Parties.** Among the political parties that had appeared on the scene by the turn of the century was the Socialist Revolutionary party, an offspring of the former Populist party. This was a clandestine organization which advocated a freely elected constituent assembly to determine the future political order of Russia, and which urged socialization of all lands for distribution among the landless peasants. Another party was the Marxist Social-Democratic party representing industrial workers. It was formed in 1898 and split in 1903 into two factions, the Bolsheviks and the Mensheviks, or the Majority and Minority. The sorrowful lot of the peasantry and the economic depression affecting urban workers at the end of the past century favored the rise of these parties. The outbreak of war in the Far East in 1904, ending with serious military reverses, caused the passive discontent already present to become violent action.

**Crisis and War in the Far East.** The Russo-Japanese conflict was caused by a persistent expansionist policy in the Far East; already begun during the last years of the reign of Alexander II, it is best illustrated by the Trans-Siberian Railway, a venture which soon turned into far more than was originally foreseen. In 1890-91, while travelling in the Far East, Nicholas II, at that time Crown Prince, took part in the ceremonies of laying the foundation for a terminal depot at Vladivostok.

The construction of the Trans-Siberian Railway soon led to the wrenching of concessions in Manchuria. In 1896 Witte obtained permission to construct the Chinese-Eastern Railway, which would link the two parts of the Trans-Siberian railway, thereby shortening the distance by almost six hundred miles. The concession implied the maintenance of a Russian guard, which was soon to become a formidable army. The Boxer rebellion led to further ill-disguised encroachment. In 1900 Russia managed to obtain concessions in the Liaotung peninsula with the acquisition of Port Arthur as a base in the south. But after expelling Japan from Korea under the pretext of preserving Chinese territorial integrity, Russia began coveting the same prizes she had recently compelled Japan to relinquish. The tsarist government managed to gain a concession on the Yalu River for the exploitation of timber; the next objective was Korea. A small but influential group of promoters, including members of the royal household, managed to obtain concessions in Korea without the knowledge of even the Russian Foreign Office. The Japanese government protested strongly, but St. Petersburg dismissed the challenge as not serious. In vain did Witte warn against such ostrich-like conduct: Nicholas II dismissed him from his ministerial post in August, 1903. Six months later Japan, without a declaration of war, attacked Russia at Port Arthur, bringing the impending crisis to its sorrowful climax.

**National Unrest.** Difficulties of conducting war at such a distance as Manchuria were formidable, and were further enhanced by the unhealthy state of affairs within the country. Social unrest soon rocked the far-flung Empire, while terroristic activities against high government officials increased. In July, 1904, the Minister of the Interior, Plehve, was assassinated by the revolutionaries.

He was succeeded by a man of milder views, Sviatopolk-Mirsky, but by the time the latter assumed office the pace of events was so accelerated that he was as much out of step with the times as was his unfortunate predecessor. The unrest reached its culmination on the memorable "Bloody Sunday" of January 22, 1905, when thousands of workers and their families, led by a priest, Gapon, marched to the Winter Palace in hopes of pleading directly with Nicholas II. But instead of the Emperor the demonstrators faced heavily armed guards, with whom they soon clashed over some unknown issue. The result was several thousand casualties, followed by increased violence, a new hopelessness of coming to any peaceful agreement with the Crown, the assassination of the Governor-General of Moscow, Grand Duke Sergei, and widespread strikes. The government became panicky and hastened to promise the summoning of a national assembly, though it did not make clear the exact purpose this assembly might serve. The specter of revolution was hovering low: the working class in the cities was now joined by a rebellious peasantry, who together constituted a grave danger to the old regime.

The First Revolution. The month of October, 1905, marked the height of the revolutionary upsurge. It was also during this month (on the 26th day) that the Council of Workers' Deputies, or Soviet, made its first appearance in the capital. This Council was made up of a few score men representing the striking workers. Shortly afterwards, similar councils were formed elsewhere in the country. The Council at St. Petersburg had every intention of turning the economic motivation of the strike into a political one: for this reason the Council insisted upon the summoning of a national representative assembly. In the midst of this crisis Witte was recalled to form a new government. He believed that the only answer would be to accede to moderate demands and grant a representative form of government.

Autocracy Makes Concessions. On October 30 the famous October Manifesto was issued: though reaffirming the inviolability of autocracy, the crown yielded to the demand for an elected legislative assembly. The Cabinet was also reformed along more modern lines, and Witte assumed the premiership. Simultaneously, the gov-

ernment proclaimed the granting of civil liberties to the
nation. This was a political move to alienate the extreme
left, who sought a social revolution, from the moderate
elements, who under present conditions might be willing
to cooperate with the government. When, however, the
moderates refused Witte's offer, he could do nothing else
but seek assistance from the old bureaucracy.

In retrospect, the events of 1905 can be considered the
prelude to the 1917 revolution. Historically speaking, the
October 1905 developments constitute the twilight of the
Russian monarchy. Autocracy won in the end, and political concessions which the crown was compelled to make
gradually reduced it to a parliamentary government fet-
tered by "fundamental" laws. Yet the fact remains that
some form of public legislature, the Duma, did emerge. It
survived until 1917, managing to outlive the monarchy,
and even succeeded in passing on authority to the initial
revolutionary government.

**The Old Regime Survives.** As autocracy began its
gradual comeback, it grew bolder. By the middle of
December, 1905, the hastily formed Soviet was banned
and most of its members were either placed under arrest
or dispersed. The revolution was reaching its low ebb—
a fact best demonstrated by the failure to call another
general strike or to form a new Soviet elsewhere, and
by the crushing of an uprising in Moscow during the
same month. This gave greater confidence to the government, which now seized the initiative in regaining its lost
position. The immediate intention was to carry out an
election for the Duma, or Parliament. In the forthcoming
election four parties came to play a prominent part: the
Socialist Revolutionaries, the Social Democrats, the
Cadets, and the Octobrists. The elections were held in
March, 1906, resulting in a considerable victory for the
parties opposing the government. Of these the Cadets
won the largest number of seats: 178 out of 524. On May
23, Nicholas II, in person, opened the first session of the
newly elected Russian Parliament. But the government, as
if to check some of those who might be carried away by
the festive occasion, announced the Fundamental Laws
on the very same day. From the outset the Laws introduced a note of anomaly—a situation wherein a parlia-

mentary government was presumably to function side by side with an adamant autocracy.

**A Political Anomaly.** The situation was even more baffling because of the fact that the executive disclaimed any responsibility to the recently formed legislative branch. Thus, in a parliamentary government the sole responsibility of the Cabinet was to the Crown. The Duma had nothing to say about the nation's external affairs, the latter being exclusively within the executive sphere. The legislature had only very limited control over the national budget; military appropriations and the maintenance of the court were exclusive functions of the Crown. The State Council served as a Upper Chamber. Half of its members were appointed by the Emperor, the other half by the zemstvos and various members of the upper class. The State Council enjoyed powers equal to those granted the Duma, and any new law had to have the consent of both chambers. The Emperor stood fully armed against both legislative chambers with Article 87 of the Fundamental Laws, which gave the executive sweeping powers to legislate by decree while the legislative body was not in session.

**The First Duma.** From its initial step the Duma faced an impasse: the leading parties assumed that, as members of parliament, they enjoyed prerogatives similar to those in corresponding institutions elsewhere. The Cabinet, on the other hand, denied any such claim, recognized only the right of interpellation, and invalidated any vote of censure. The Duma locked horns with the Cabinet ministers over the latter issue, and the Crown finally dissolved the adamant legislature in the hope that another election might bring a more coöperative majority. Several favorable developments gave the Crown assurance. The government had successfully concluded negotiations with France for a huge loan—over two billion francs—in spite of protests and warnings to France from the opposition, which could foresee serious political repercussions. If the loan were contracted, it would bolster the monarchy by enabling the tsarist government to attain stability and carry out its policies independently, disregarding the opinion of the legislature. The dissolution of the Duma forced the opposition to gather hastily at

Viborg and issue an appeal in the form of a Manifesto, signed by some two hundred members, urging the nation to pay no taxes and send no men into the army until the government revoked the dissolution decree. But the appeal had no effect.

**Stolypin's Reforms.** At this stage Nicholas II asked Peter Stolypin, Minister of the Interior, to assume the post of Premier. A moderate conservative with an iron will, fearless, and with a scope of vision confined to national rather than continental affairs, Stolypin nonetheless pursued his aims with almost brutal conviction and clarity. Shortly after he took office the elections to the second Duma were held. Stolypin hoped that the newly elected legislature body would approve his program of "First pacification then reforms," which called for a policy of relentless repression along with agrarian reforms that would result in greater stability throughout the country.

As a small land owner and former governor in the Volga region, Stolypin believed that the only measure to restore public order and political stability would be a solution to the agrarian problem. To this end he first turned his attention to the peasant commune, which had been sentimentally revered by some nationalists, condemned by others, and utitilized by the government since 1861 for its own administrative purposes. Stolypin had his own reasons for re-examining the role of the commune; he concluded that it had outlived its purpose, that its obsolete character served more as an impediment to sound agricultural management than as a stimulant to social security. With characteristic determination he resolved to end the antiquated social organization. Instead of collective ownership, Stolypin advocated the need for a strong peasantry based on individual land ownership; he counted on the peasants' acquisitive instincts and strong sense of proprietorship rather than their shaky loyalty to the communal principle. The individual peasant, Stolypin believed, would form a conservative element in the country, loyal to the monarchy, inimical to revolution, and immune to subversive propaganda, hence the backbone of national stability.

Consequently, in November, 1905, redemption payments were discontinued while the commune ceased its functions; each member was given the choice of either remaining voluntarily within the commune or departing it. A year later a law was passed stating that in case two-thirds of a rural community voted in favor of consolidating their individual strips into a single private landholding, the resolution must be enforced. Though communes continued in many parts of Russia, the area of communal lands and their membership declined annually. Between 1908 and 1909 Russia witnessed a rapid transformation of its old agrarian social order. At the outbreak of the first world war, about a fourth of the peasants converted their communal property into private holdings, while one in ten consolidated the separate strips of communal land into single permanent personal holdings.

**The Second Duma.** The second Duma unpleasantly surprised the government, which faced a stronger opposition bloc there than in the previous Duma. The Socialist Revolutionary and Laborite parties gained considerable ground at the expense of the moderate parties. Stolypin, losing patience, urged the Crown to dissolve the Duma again and to hold another election only after altering the electoral law. For all practical purposes this was an absolute violation of the law, but so determined was Stolypin to attain his goal that he cared little for its legality. His first aim was to locate the source from which the opposing parties drew their support, then curb their representation. Various schemes and manipulations were employed: removing all possible influence from national minority groups, granting additional voting power to the gentry, revising the voting districts. These stratagems paid off well, for the third election appreciably reduced the strength of the opposition parties while simultaneously securing the Octobrist party, which was willing to coöperate with the government, about a third of the seats of the Duma.

**The Third Duma.** Stolypin meanwhile was busy with "pacification" of the country. Taking advantage of the notorious Article 87, which allowed the executive emergency legislation while the Duma was not in session, he proceeded to carry out his land reforms and a repression campaign against subversive elements throughout the country, by specially created courts. When the third Duma met, it approved the entire program and Stolypin's

triumph was complete. The third Duma nearly completed
its full five-year term, and the fourth one, elected in
1912, proved even more conservative. By this time, however, the strong guiding hand of Stolypin was no longer
at the helm, for Stolypin had been assassinated in Kiev
in September, 1911. The monarchy was slowly drifting
toward its end, particularly from the outbreak of war
in the summer of 1914.

**Recovery.** The period between 1907 and 1914 marks
a rather impressive record of accomplishment. Though
one might discern undermining political factors, particularly at the top level of officialdom, nonetheless in the
country at large it was also possible to detect salutary
signs. Whatever one might think of its weaknesses, a
legislature did emerge to serve as a constant reminder
that Russia had an elected assembly. It was equally difficult to overlook the profound social changes in the rural
areas. Simultaneously, Russia had been making impressive technological progress and carrying through important social legislation. All told, the reforms contributed
to a stability which Russia had not seen for some time.
Political and economic stabilization was partly due to the
enervating effects of revolutionary events, and particularly the triumph of the monarchy, upon the public; it
could be attributed partly to the acceptance of a belief in
slower evolutionary—rather than speedier, though less
certain, revolutionary—means. Standards of living were
gradually improved, while local government could boast
of the setting up of a net of consumers' cooperatives, an
organization for public health, the founding of many public schools, and effective application of science to agriculture. Trade unions were still outlawed, yet social legislation improved the wage scale and provided sickness and
accident insurance. Perhaps the most notable advance
was in the field of education: on the eve of the war in
1914, about fifty per cent of children between seven and
fourteen years of age attended school. That strife occurred again in the land could be ascribed very largely to
economic rather than political factors.

**War Paves the Road to Revolution.** The war years
brought, along with many hardships, the specter of revolution again. At the outbreak of the war there was a
tremendous outburst of patriotic sentiment; but as the

weary months continued, the prospect of peace seemed
more and more remote. Shortly after the outbreak of
war, Russia suffered such a disastrous military defeat at
Tannenberg that only a country with such enormous
resources of manpower could have endured without total
collapse. If the disaster saved France, it meant potential
danger within its own national confines. Deprivations and
sufferings seemed endless, intensifying the danger of
social and political unrest.

Despite all military reforms, the army was far from
being prepared to participate in a war of such long duration. There were appalling shortages of food and ammunition, catastrophic technological backwardness, and con-
spicuous inferiority of leadership. There was only one
commodity in profusion—manpower—though the soldiers were poorly equipped and disheartened by frequent
defeats. Desertion soon increased. The strangest aspect of
this lamentable development was the fact that the government feared public initiative regardless of the patriotic
motivation. Autocracy had no experience in delegating
initiative to the general public. Various organizations
were eager to put their shoulders to the wheel of state:
the Duma, the zemstvos, the various municipal organizations, all offered readily to contribute their share, but the
government would rather have faced disaster.

During the war the Duma seldom met and then only
at the caprice of the sovereign. It would meet for a short
session and then be quickly prorogued while the government ruled the country in accordance with Article 87.
Constantinople and the Straits had been dangling before
Russia as an enticing prize of victory; but as months
went by and the losses kept mounting, even the long-
cherished hope of replacing the crescent with the cross
over St. Sophia could no longer inspire valor. By the end
of 1915 Russia lost all of Poland, much of the Baltic
coast, White Russia, and a large portion of the Ukraine.
In view of such territorial losses the middle-of-the-road
parties formed in the Duma a "Progressive bloc." Its aim
was to force on the government the formation of a Cabinet that might enjoy national confidence. The Progressive bloc insisted that the government must improve its
public relations if it expected to win the war.

The Emperor, meanwhile, did little except to assume

responsibilities beyond his official capacity or personal ability. He became commander-in-chief of the armed forces, which was a fatal error: henceforth the responsibility for all reverses was placed upon his feeble shoulders. (*See Readings Nos. 15 and 16.*) While Nicholas II devoted his entire time to General Headquarters, the government fell even more under the influence of the Tsarina in the capital. Entirely inept, frustrated, hysterical, she had only one ambition: to see that her only son inherited the throne. As the savior of the royal heir, Rasputin became more than ever the indispensable and holy man whose counsel was not to be questioned.

**The Role of Rasputin.** Rasputin's part in the last years of the monarchy can hardly be comprehended unless one understands the mental state of the Tsarina. Rasputin, an illiterate, profligate Siberian peasant, managed to exert a truly destructive influence upon the Empress through his hypnotic personality. Anyone falling from Rasputin's grace was politically doomed. Whether one accepted or rejected Rasputin became a matter of political life and death: the fate of the Empire was literally in his hands. Cabinets came and went, policies were adopted and discarded only at the whim of Rasputin. The "Holy Man" began offering his counsel even on matters pertaining to military strategy. (*See Readings Nos. 17 and 18.*)

Appalling casualties at the front and the critical economic condition at home were bound cumulatively to undermine the entire imperial structure. The war wreaked unbelievable havoc upon Russia. The blockade of Russian ports by the Central Powers had a serious effect upon trade: transportation was crippled and the cities were the first to feel the devastating effects of grave shortages of food and fuel. The cost of living rose continually. The countryside, too, felt the effects of the war: not only did the rise in living costs affect rural life, but the heavy drain in manpower proved a grave deterrent to agriculture. Whatever the peasant did manage to produce he was reluctant to yield to the government as long as he was paid in the increasingly depreciated currency.

**Revolution From Above Fails.** Schemes of a palace revolution were floating about the capital for some time during 1916. As the political muddle continued, as one military failure followed another, and as Rasputin continued to tamper with state affairs, a louder cry arose for drastic action. This was further necessitated by a rumor that Rasputin favored Russia's withdrawal from the war and the signing of a separate peace with the Central Powers. Discontent with the unhealthy state of court life led to the assassination of Rasputin on December 30, 1916, at the home of Prince Youssoupoff. This was no revolutionary act, but a desperate measure to forestall revolution and save the monarchy. (*See Readings Nos. 18 and 19.*) Along with this belated act of violence came hopeful schemes such as to persuade the Emperor to resign as commander-in-chief, or to form a new Cabinet chosen for ability and integrity rather than loyalty to Rasputin. Nicholas would not listen to any suggestions except those of his wife. Early in March, 1917, violence began to break out in the capital. The food queues lengthened; the workers became more restless and ready to strike; the troops in Petrograd could not be relied upon in case of public disorders. The Empire was speedily moving toward its doom. As days went by, accumulated impatience, discontent, and protest led to clashes with authority. The summoned troops were themselves ready to join those whom they were supposed to quell. The revolution was in the making.

Abdication. Between the tottering government and the rising populace stood the shadowy body of the Duma. It was this assembly that confirmed the organization of a provisional government headed by a man closely associated with the zemstvos, Prince Lvov. The newly formed government consisted of moderate liberals, with the exception only of Kerensky, a socialist of the right wing. With the formation of the Provisional Government the Revolution began. On March 15, the next logical step took place: Nicholas II finally yielded, and on his own behalf as well as that of his son he submitted to abdication in favor of his brother, the Grand Duke Michael. When the latter declined to accept the throne unless the offer was presented to him by a freely elected assembly, the monarchy sentenced itself to death. (*See Readings Nos. 20 and 21.*) The Provisional Government had thus no choice but to assume entire responsibility for the duration of the war or until a Constituent Assembly had been summoned to make its final choice.

**The Tragic End.** The Romanov dynasty ended on July 16, 1918, when the entire royal family perished in the basement of the home of their confinement at Ekaterinburg. (*See Reading No. 22.*) The Romanovs had ascended the Russian throne in 1613, after a fifteen-year social revolution that swept the country from border to border; the dynasty ended after 304 years in the midst of another revolution, the historic significance of which can be at present only vaguely perceived.

# Part II
## READINGS

— Reading No. 1 —

# KLYUCHEVSKY ON REASONS FOR ELECTION OF THE ROMANOV CANDIDATE

*The most distinguished Russian historian, V. O. Klyu-chevsky, offers sound reasons for the election of the Romanov candidate to the vacant throne of Russia—not because he was the "most capable," but the "most convenient" one. (From V. O. Klyuchevsky, A History of Russia, vol. III, pp. 61-63, New York: E. P. Dutton & Co., 1913.)*

Thus the election of Michael by the Council was both engineered and confirmed in the Council and among the people by a series of subsidiary methods, by preliminary agitation with the help of the numerous Romanov family, by pressure from a Cossack force, by secret inquisition among the masses, and by the acclamations of a metropolitan mob in the Red Square. Yet these electoral devices proved successful only because they were supported by the relation of the community to one great house in particular. Michael attained victory, not through personal or propagandist, but through purely family, popularity. He belonged to a boyar stock which was one of the most beloved of the Muscovite public—the Romanovs being a recent offshoot of the old boyar house of the Koshkins. As early as the reign of Ivan Kalita (1328-1340) there arrived in Moscow from what the *Rodoslovetz* [Genealogical Almanac] calls "the Land of Prus" a noble who, in the Muscovite capital, subsequently became known as Andrei Ivanovich Kobuila [Kobyla]. He later rose to be a leading boyar at the Muscovite court, and from his fifth son, Theodore Koshka, there sprang the clan of the Koshkins, who flourished at the Muscovite court throughout the fourteenth and fifteenth centuries. They constituted the only non-titled boyar family to remain non-submerged by the stream of new titled servitors which flooded Moscow from the middle of the fifteenth century onwards; yet even among such men as the Princes Shuiski, Vorotinski and Mstislavski the Koshkins still maintained their place in the front rank of boyardom. Now, at the beginning of the sixteenth century a boyar named Roman Yurevich Zacharin (who was descended from a grandson of the original Koshka, named Zachariah) was occupying a leading position at court: and it was he who became the founder of the new branch of that family—the branch of the Romanovs. Of his sons, again Nikita (own brother to the Tsaritsa Anastasia (first wife of Ivan IV) is remarkable for having been the only Muscovite boyar of the sixteenth century to leave behind him a grateful memory among the people. Indeed, we find his name commemorated in a popular *bilina*, or folksong, of the time of Ivan IV, which depicts him as acting as a sort of benevolent intermediary between the nation and its choleric Tsar. Finally, of Nikita's six sons the most prominent was the eldest, Theodor, who was a gentle, kind-hearted boyar, a dandy, and a great lover of learning. The Englishman Horsey, then resident in Moscow, relates in his memoirs that Theodor was very desirous of acquiring the Latin language, and that, at his request, Horsey compiled for him a Latin grammar in which the Latin words were written in Russian characters. The persecution which the Nikitisches suffered under the suspicious Godunov—as well as their personal qualities—undoubtedly contributed to the popularity of the Romanovs. Palitsin even goes so far as to place this persecution among the three sins for which God punished the Russian land during the Period of Troubles. Also, their feud with Tsar Shuiski and their connection with Tushino obtained for the Romanovs the protection of the second false Dimitri, and also popularity in the Cossack camps: whence the family's equivocal bearing during the Period of Troubles won for Michael a double amount of support, both in the provinces and among the Cossacks. What most assisted him, however, in the election in Council was the blood tie which existed between the Romanovs and the old dynasty. During the Troubles Period the Russian nation so often erred in its choice of new Tsars that at length it came to look upon no election as lasting which did not fall upon a person connected—no matter how—with the pristine house of Tsars. Consequently in Michael the nation beheld, not the chosen candidate of the Council, but a nephew of Tsar Theodor, who himself had been a "born" or hereditary Tsar. Indeed, an annalist of the day says that men desiderated Michael for the throne "by reason of his union of kindred with the magnificent Tsars." Again, Palitsin calls Michael "the chosen of God before birth," while Timotheev places him in an unbroken line of hereditary Tsars, and next to Theodor (thus ignoring Godunov, Shuiski, and the various pretenders). Moreover, Michael himself, in his memoirs, calls Ivan IV his grandfather. Finally, it is a moot question whether Michael was not helped to election by a current rumor that, when dying, Tsar Theodor orally bequeathed the throne to his cousin Theodor, Michael's father. At all events the boyars (who supervised the elections in Council) may well have been inclined in Michael's favour by another recommendation—a recommendation which they could not afford to disregard. An item exists that a certain Sheremetev wrote to Prince Golitzin, in Poland, the words: "Our Michael is as yet but young, and hath not come unto understanding: yet is he such a one as will be familiar unto us." This can only mean that, though Sheremetev knew that the throne would not deprive Michael of the power of maturing, or render his youth a permanent condition, other qualities in the land presaged the fact that the nephew would resemble the uncle (Tsar Theodor) in point of mental and physical debility, and would thus develop into a gentle, kind-hearted Tsar under whom the trials endured by the boyars during the reigns of Ivan IV and Boris Godunov would never be repeated. In short, it was not the most *capable*, but the most *convenient*, Tsar that was the need of the hour.

Thus the founder of a new dynasty appeared to put an end to the Period of Troubles.

# ALEXIS, SECOND TSAR OF THE ROMANOV LINE

*From V. O. Klyuchevsky,* A History of Russia, *vol. III, ch. 16.*

✓　　　✓　　　✓

Tsar Alexis was born in 1629, and traversed the whole curriculum of ancient Russian education—of what was known as "the teaching of letters.". . . By the time Alexis was eleven or twelve he possessed a small library which, composed chiefly of gifts from his grandfather, his uncles, and his tutor, numbered thirteen volumes. For the most part the tomes consisted of copies of Holy Writ and the Church's service-books, but among them were figured also a grammar which had been printed in Lithuania, a cosmography, and a lexicon of some sort which likewise hailed from the Lithuanian country. In the literary connection the Tsarevitch's head instructor was the boyar B. I. Morozov, who was a leading member of the aristocracy, and strongly attached to the learning of Western Europe. This man introduced into the curriculum of the young Alexis a system of ocular instruction. —*i.e.* he familiarised him with various subjects through means of German engravings; while a still more daring innovation which he introduced into the Muscovite palace of State was to clothe the Tsarevitch and his young brother in German costume.

Arrived at maturity, Alexis presented an exceedingly attractive combination of the good qualities of the old-time Russian who remained true to antiquity with the leanings of a man for whom useful and pleasant novelties had a powerful attraction. A model of piety—of that measured, ever-studied godliness to which the religious sense of ancient Rus devoted so much time and attention

—he could argue with any monk on the subject of prayer and fasting; and during the seasons of Lent and the Assumption he observed Sundays, Tuesdays, Thursdays, and Saturdays by partaking of one meal a day (at which his food consisted only of cabbage-soup, mushrooms, and berries—never of meat), while on Mondays, Wednesdays, and Fridays he ate and drank nothing at all. Also, he would spend periods of five or six hours in church—making, on some days, a thousand obeisances, and, on other days, fifteen hundred. In short, he was a true "religious" who, in his efforts to save his soul, combined bodily toil with tense exercise of the religious sense. This piety had a potent effect both upon his governmental ideas and his everyday relations. . . .

. . . Tsar Alexis was a man of the purest loving-kindness; he was the best type of Russian. Indeed, I see in him the finest figure which ancient Rus ever produced, for I know no other character who could have produced so pleasing an impression, *had he not been the occupant of the throne.* For the latter position he was too passive a character. Nature or his upbringing led to the development in him of the very qualities which are most valued in the round of daily life, and impart so much light and warmth to domestic relations. Yet, for all his quickness of moral perception, Alexis lacked sufficient *moral energy* . . . . Too feeble, or too little disposed, to persist in or to carry through a given matter, or to contend with anyone for long, he would appoint to important posts not only gifted and honorable agents, but also men upon whom he himself set the lowest value. . . .

It befell this Tsar to have to withstand the impact of some very important internal and external movements. During his reign all relations—relations old, and of recent birth; relations with Sweden, Poland, the Crimean, Turkey, and Western Rus; relations social and ecclesiastical—became accentuated, thrown into opposition, and confused; they gave birth to insistent questions which called for an answer, without any regard to their historical order. Finally, over them all, as the key to their general resolution, towered the fundamental question: Are we to remain true to native antiquity, or are we to take lessons of the foreigner? . . .

# PETER'S JOURNEY TO ENGLAND IN 1698

*Gilbert Burnet (1643-1715) was a noted English bishop and historian. Among his writings stands out his* History of My Own Time, *a work begun in 1685. A keen observer and witness of Peter's memorable visit to England, his account merits special attention. The story refers to Peter's journey to England in 1698.*

╱          ╱          ╱

He [Peter I] came this winter over to England and stayed some months among us. I waited often on him, and was ordered both by the king and the archbishop and bishops to attend upon him and to offer him such informations of our religion and constitution as he was willing to receive. I had good interpreters, so I had much free discourse with him. He is a man of a very hot temper, soon inflamed and very brutal in his passion. He raises his natural heat by drinking much brandy, which he rectifies himself with great application. He is subject to convulsive motions all over his body, and his head seems to be affected with these. He wants not capacity, and has a larger measure of knowledge than might be expected from his education, which was very indifferent. A want of judgment, with an instability of temper, appear in him too often and too evidently.

He is mechanically turned, and seems designed by nature rather to be a ship carpenter than a great prince. This was his chief study and exercise while he stayed here. He wrought much with his own hands and made all about him work at the models of ships. He told me he designed a great fleet at Azuph [Azov] and with it to attack the Turkish empire. But he did not seem capable of conducting so great a design, though his conduct in his wars since this has discovered a greater genius in him than appeared at this time.

He was desirous to understand our doctrine, but he did not seem disposed to mend matters in Muscovy. He was, indeed, resolved to encourage learning and to polish his people by sending some of them to travel in other countries and to draw strangers to come and live among them. He seemed apprehensive still of his sister's intrigues. There was a mixture both of passion and severity in his temper. He is resolute, but understands little of war, and seemed not at all inquisitive that way.

After I had seen him often, and had conversed much with him, I could not but adore the depth of the providence of God that had raised up such a furious man to so absolute an authority over so great a part of the world. . . .

He went from hence to the court of Vienna, where he purposed to have stayed some time, but he was called home sooner than he had intended upon a discovery, or a suspicion, of intrigues managed by his sister. The strangers, to whom he trusted most, were so true to him that those designs were crushed before he came back. But on this occasion he let loose his fury on all whom he suspected. Some hundreds of them were hanged all around Moskow, and it was said that he cut off many heads with his own hands; and so far was he from relenting or showing any sort of tenderness that he seemed delighted with it. How long he is to be the scourge of that nation God only knows.

— Reading No. 4 —

# SOPHIA CHARLOTTE ON PETER I

*Among many historians of the reign of Peter I the name of the American writer Eugene Schuyler is undoubtedly the best known. Before Schuyler had completed his two-volume history of* Peter the Great *(1884), the author must have examined an enormous number of sources available in his day. The result of his labor is a biography of the illustrious sovereign that still makes profitable reading. Below is a letter of Sophia Charlotte, wife of the Elector of Brandenburg, cited by Eugene Schuyler.*

✓        ✓        ✓

The Tsar [Peter I] is very tall, his features are fine, and his figure very noble. He has great vivacity of mind, and a ready and just repartee. But with all the advantages with which nature has endowed him, it could be wished that his manners were a little less rustic. We immediately sat down to table. Herr Koppenstein, who did the duty of marshal, presented the napkin to his Majesty, who was greatly embarrassed, for at Brandenburg, instead of a table-napkin, they had given him an ewer and basin after the meal. He was very gay, very talkative, and we established a great friendship for each other, and he exchanged snuff-boxes with my daughter. We stayed, in truth, a very long time at table, but we would gladly have remained there long still without feeling a moment of *ennui,* for the Tsar was in very good humour, and never ceased talking to us. My daughter had her Italians sing. Their song pleased him, though he confessed to us that he did not care much for music.

I asked him if he liked hunting. He replied that his father had been very fond of it, but that he himself, from his earliest youth, had had a real passion for navigation ships, showed us his hands, and made us touch the callous places that had been caused by work. He brought his musicians, and they played Russian dances, which he liked better than Polish ones.

Lefot and his nephew dressed in French style, and had much wit. We did not speak to the other ambassadors. We regretted that he could not stay longer, so that we could see him again, for his society gave us much pleasure. He is a very extraordinary man. It is impossible to describe him, or even to give an idea of him, unless you have seen him. He has a very good heart, and remarkably noble sentiments. I must tell you, also, that he did not get drunk in our presence, but we had hardly left when the people of his suite made ample amends."

In another letter Sophia Charlotte refers again to Peter:
"I could embellish the tale of the journey of the illustrious Tsar, if I should tell you that he is sensible to the
charms of beauty, but, to come to the bare fact, I found
in him no disposition of gallantry. If we had not taken
so many steps to see him, I believe that he would never
have thought of us. In his country it is the custom for all
women to paint, and rouge forms an essential part of
their marriage presents. That is why Countess Platen
singularly pleased the Muscovites; but in dancing, they
took the whalebones of our corsets for our bones, and the
Tsar showed his astonishment by saying that the German
ladies had devilish hard bones.

They have four dwarfs. Two of them are very well-pro-
portioned, and perfectly well-bred; sometimes he kissed,
and sometimes he pinched the ear of his favorite dwarf.
He took the head of our little Princess [Sophia Dorothea,
ten years old], and kissed her twice. The ribbons of her
hair suffered in consequence. He also kissed her brother
[afterwards George II, of England, then sixteen years old].
He is a prince at once very good and very *méchant*. He
has quite the manners of his country. If he had received
a better education, he would be an accomplished man,
for he has many good qualities, and an infinite amount
of natural wit.

— Reading No. 5 —

# MANSTEIN ON THE EVENTS OF 1727-44

*General C. H. de Manstein served in the Russian army
during the reign of Anne (1730-40). With the accession
of Elizabeth his position became precarious on account
of the rising anti-German feelings. Information reached
the authorities of Manstein's disloyalty; however, a court*

*martial found him innocent, but he never regained the former prestige he had enjoyed. In 1744 he escaped to Prussia where he wrote his Memoirs. After his defection, General Manstein was tried in absentia and sentenced to death.*

*Familiar with conditions in Russia, particularly with Russian court life, and well versed in the language, Manstein left to posterity a rare document that faithfully records events during the years 1727-44. The Memoirs were originally written in German, and later, at the request of Frederick II, rendered into French; then into English. Eventually the Memoirs of Manstein were translated into more than a dozen languages.* (C. H. de Manstein, Memoirs of Russia, Historical, Political, and Military, from 1727 to 1744, *London, 1770, pp. 26-28.*)

✓ ✓ ✓

The council of state, the senate, and such of the principal generals of the army as were then at Moscow, assembled immediately after the decease of Peter II and sat in close committee in a chamber of the palace of Kremlin. The high-chancellor Golofkin announced to the assembly the death of the Emperor, and as soon as he had done speaking, the Prince Demetrius Michaelowitz Gallitzin got up, and said, that "since, *by the demise of Peter II. the whole male line of Peter I. was extinct, and that Russia had suffered extremely by despotic power, to the prevalence of which the great number of foreigners brought in by Peter I. had greatly contributed, it would be highly expedient to limit the supreme authority by salutary laws, and not to confer the imperial crown on the new Empress that should be chosen, but under certain conditions;"* concluding with putting the question to the whole assembly, *whether "they did not approve this proposal?"* They all assented to it, without any of the least opposition. Upon which the Prince Basilius Loukitsch Dolgoroucki proposed the duchess dowager of Courland; alleging, that the crown was now falling to female, it was but just to prefer the daughter of the Czar Iwan, the elder brother of Peter I. to those of this Emperor; that though the duchess of Mecklenburgh was the eldest, it was to be considered that she was married to a foreign Prince, whereas the Duchess of Courland was actually a widow, and, not being above thirty-six years of age, might marry and give heirs to Russia.

The true reason, however, for preferring the duchess of Courland was, that she being at Mittau, the remoteness of that place would afford time for firmer establishment of the republican system.

All the votes then united in her favor, and it was agreed that the council of state, which was at that time constituted of seven members, of whom the majority were the Dolgorouckis or their relations, should have the whole power, and the assembly framed the following articles:

*1st.* That the Empress Anne was to reign only in virtue of the resolves, upon deliberation of the privy-council.

*2d.* That she should not declare war nor make peace on her own authority.

*3d.* That she would not lay any new tax, or bestow any post or place of consequence.

*4th.* That she would punish no gentleman with death unless he was duly convicted of his crime.

*5th.* That she should not confiscate anyone's property.

*6th.* That she should not alienate or dispose of any lands belonging to the crown.

*7th.* That she should not marry, nor choose an heir, without asking, upon all these points, the consent of the privy-council.

The assembly then chose three members to notify to the Empress of her accession to the throne, and to propose to her the conditions under which she should reign.

On the part of the council was deputed the Prince Basilius Loukitsch Dolgoroucki; on the part of the senate, the Prince Michael Galitzin; and on the part of the nobility, the lieutenant-general Leontev.

In the instructions given to the deputies, it was enjoined to them, to require of the Empress that she should sign the above articles, and that she should not bring her favorite with her to Moscow, Biren, gentleman of the chamber.

# BAIN'S ACCOUNT OF ELIZABETH

*Robert Nisbet Bain was a librarian by profession, employed in the British Museum. History to Bain was a hobby and for this reason his writings are noted for favorite heroes and events. His narratives are noted neither for lucidity nor organization of material. Events, big and small, are casually and indiscriminately piled together. And still, amidst the bulky material gathered by the author one is liable to locate haphazardly scattered citations from rare documents and flashes of penetrating interpretations. An excellent linguist, Bain was able to utilize many sources inaccessible to others. Following is part of a masterful account of Elizabeth from* The Daughter of Peter the Great: A History of Russian Diplomacy and of the Russian Court Under the Empress Elizabeth Petrovna, 1741-1762, *New York, E. P. Dutton & Co., 1900.*

↑        ↑        ↑

. . . In the summer [Elizabeth] hawked and hunted, and, in winter, took horse exercise in the vast covered riding-school built in the reign of Anne for the favourite Biren. She was an excellent shot, a fearless and graceful rider, and could, in her best days, outwalk the strongest of her guardsmen. Nor was she altogether without aesthetic tastes, being passonately fond of music and the drama, and taking a great interest in architecture. No other Russian Sovereign ever erected so many churches, and the celebrated Winter Palace, Rastrelli's masterpiece, was built under her supervision, though she did not live long enough to inhabit it.

But building was by no means her most costly pastime. For every hundred rubles she expended on the permanent embellishment of her capital, she wasted a thousand on

the transitory pleasures of her Court. Lavish to the verge
of extravagance, and loving pomp and show with all the
ardour of a sensuous semi-barbarous Oriental, it was the
great delight of Elizabeth Petrovna to pose as the majestic
central figure of brilliant assemblies and gorgeous pag-
eants, and her court was indisputably the most splendid
in Europe. Her cousin Anne, before her, had indeed
astonished foreigners by the gorgeousness of her appointments, but Anne's crude and bizarre magnificence lacked
the veneer of grace, elegance and refinement which characterized the court of Elizabeth. For, though in many
respects a Russian gentlewoman of the old school, and
intensely patriotic, Elizabeth Petrovna was far more in-
telligent and receptive than Anne Ivanovna, and, especially where her pleasures were concerned, borrowed
freely from the luxuries of the Western civilization. Hence
the accusation of reckless extravagance. . . . This extravagance manifested itself principally in the habiliments,
equipages, retinue and banquets of the gentry and nobility,
the Empress herself setting the example in this respect.
She is said to have changed her clothes half-a-dozen
times a day, and although she lost 4,000 dresses at the
great Moscow conflagration in 1747, fifteen thousand
more were found in her wardrobes after her death, most
of which had only been worn once. And the Empress took
care that her courtiers should live up to this high standard
of display. At the wedding of the Grand Duke Peter, all
public officials were given a year's salary in advance that
they might be able to make a brave show on the occasion,
and a special ukaze laid down sumptuary regulations for
the pageant. Every member of the first and second class in
the table of grades was to have two Heydukes and not
less than eight lackeys attached to each of his carriages,
and as many more as he could afford. But the *jeunesse
dorée* of Peterhof and Tsarskoe Selo needed little prompt-
ing. Their natural vanity and luxuriousness met the Tsaritsa's wishes half way. It soon became the ambition of
every young Russian noble to outshine his neighbour,
and at last even the most expensive galloon was generally
looked down upon as common and vulgar. Sergius Na-
ruishkin, accounted the greatest dandy of the age in
Russia, won great favour by going to the wedding of
the Grand Duke, in a carriage inlaid all over, even to

the wheels, with crystal mirrors, and wearing a caftan ablaze with jewels, the back of which was made to imitate a tree, the trunk being represented by a broad golden band in the middle of his body, while the branches were indicated by lines of silver running up the sleeves to the wrists, and the roots by similar lines running down to the knees of the breeches. . . . Then there was Field Marshal Stephen Apraksin who had hundreds of suits of clothes, a jewelled snuff-box for every day in the year, and required more than five hundred horses to drag his private baggage when he took the field against the King of Prussia; and Count Peter Borisovich Sheremetev, the richest man in the Empire, whose dresses were heavy with gold and silver, and who always went about surrounded by a whole army of domestics almost as brilliantly attired as himself. It is recorded of him that he kept such an ample table that once, when the Empress and her by no means tiny court looked in upon him unawares, he was able to entertain them all sumptuously with what was actually provided for the use of his household on that particular day. The lesser nobles naturally imitated the magnates, and the result was a rapid declension from the simplicity of the old Russian mode of life, and a growing fondness for costly and unnecessary exotic luxuries which ministered to vanity and dissipation with often the most serious consequences. This was bad enough, but still worse remained behind, for the Court of Elizabeth was not only the most extravagant, it was also the most licentious in Europe, and for this also the Empress must be held primarily responsible.


— Reading No. 7 —

# BAIN'S ACCOUNT OF PETER III

*Perhaps the best known of Robert Nisbet Bain's historical works is* Peter III Emperor of Russia: The Story of a Crisis and a Crime (*Westminster: Archibald Con-*

*stable & Co., 1902). The following is a biographical account of Peter III as given by Mr. Bain. (Pp. 1-24 passim.)*

On February 21st, 1728, the young consort of Charles Frederick, Duke of Holstein, was brought to bed of a son, who, on the following day, in the Lutheran church at Kiel, was christened Charles Peter Ulric. The names thus given to the lad were eloquent of his illustrious lineage. He was called Charles, like his father before him, after his paternal great-uncle Charles XII, ever the best, oftentimes the only, friend of the House of Holstein. He owed his second name, Peter, to his late grandfather, Peter the Great, while his third name, Ulric, was a compliment to his great-aunt, the actual Queen regnant of Sweden. The little gentleman, though he had in his veins the blood of heroes and empire makers, was but a puny creature at best, and Fate, who had such a strange and terrible destiny in store for him, was unkind to him from his very cradle: he lost his mother when he was only ten days old. . . .

All his life long he had been the football of Fortune. Driven from his native land by the Danes while still a youth, always either a fugitive or a pensioner, this disappointed pretender to a visionary crown had grown up a soured misanthrope. That he was peevish, obstinate, haughty, and narrow-minded, we can well believe; that his unhappy overtaxed subjects paid dearly for their master's crotchets, we know for certain; yet there was a touch of nobility in the steadfastness with which he rejected every proposal to compromise his claims upon Sleswick and Sweden, whether accompanied by threats or promises. This solitary trait of firmness of character is distinctly reminiscent of his uncle, Charles XII, who considered it a point of honour in the days of his adversity to maintain a magnificent establishment, although while still the conqueror of kings and the arbiter of Europe his contempt for pomp had been notorious. . . .

Apart from soldiering, the lad's education was of a very indifferent description, not so much in consequence of the stupidity and brutality of his teachers, as because he was the victim, from the first, of two conflicting pedagogic systems alternately and indiscriminately applied. As the nearest male relation of Peter the Great, he seemed at one time to have a fair chance of ascending the Russian throne and, accordingly, in the first instance, he received some instruction in the principles of the Russian language and the Orthodox Religion, and the Greek chapel, established at Kiel for the benefit of his mother, was retained for his use. But when, on the death of Peter II, the Muscovites, altogether ignoring the little Holstein Prince, elected Anne of Courland as Empress, there was a bitter reaction at the Court of Kiel against everything Russian, and all the hopes of the needy Holsteiners were fixed upon Sweden, whose old and childless King, Frederick of Hesse, alone stood between Charles XII's nearest blood relation and the Swedish throne. Henceforth the Muscovites were ridiculed to Charles Peter Ulric as barbarians, and he received the education best adapted for a Prince who was expected, one day, to sit upon the principal Lutheran throne of the north. . . .

↗        ↗        ↗

On the night of December 6th, 1741, his aunt, the Tsarevna Elizabeth Petrovna, at the head of the Preobrazhensky Grenadiers, overthrew the existing Russian government, and the first thing the new Empress did, on feeling securely established on her throne, was to send for her nephew, her one remaining male kinsman, whom she had already resolved to adopt as her successor. . . .

↗        ↗        ↗

. . . On the following day [July 9th, 1744], Peter and Catherine exchanged rings of betrothal in the Uspensky Cathedral, and a *Ukaz* was read in which, for the first time, Catherine was designated orthodox Grand-Duchess. From July 26th to October 1st the Court migrated to Kiev. During the course of its wanderings, the Grand Duke, who had been suffering from fainting fits all through the summer, was attacked by small-pox, and his life was, for a time, in danger. The Empress, despite the warnings of the doctors, insisted upon nursing her nephew herself, and her prayers and tears were at length rewarded by his recovery. But he was now more rickety than ever, and so hideously pock-marked that his *fiancée* could scarce endure the sight of him. No sooner was he fairly on his legs again, however, than the Empress hastened on the wedding, which took place, at St. Petersburg on August 21st, 1745 . . .

Such a union between a Prince, who, physically, was something less than a man, and mentally little more than a child, and a Princess of prodigious intellect and with an insatiable capacity for enjoyment, was bound to end in a catastrophe. . . .

— Reading No. 8 —

# CATHERINE II ON THE END OF HER DEPOSED HUSBAND

*Catherine II left to posterity many writings, but to the student of history her Memoirs, which include important historical documents such as those cited below, are of utmost importance. Here is a brief reference which Catherine II herself made concerning the sad end of her deposed husband, followed by three letters in which he pathetically appealed for mercy and freedom to leave Russia. (From* The Memoirs of Catherine the Great, *ed. by Dominique Maroger, New York: The Macmillan Company, 1955, pp. 345-46.)*

✓         ✓         ✓

. . . I sent the deposed Emperor to Ropsha, fifteen miles from Petersburg under the command of Alexis Orlov, while respectable and comfortable rooms were being prepared for him in Schlüsselburg and also to give time to organize a relay of horses.

But God disposed differently. Fright had given him a colic that lasted three days and passed on the fourth. On that day he drank excessively—for he had everything he wanted, except liberty. The illness affected his brain, it was followed by a great weakness and in spite of all the assistance of physicians, he gave up the ghost, after asking for a Lutheran priest. I had him opened up—but his stomach showed no traces of ill-health. The cause of death was established as inflammation of the bowels and apoplexy. He had an inordinately small heart, quite withered.

*[There follow three letters of Peter III to Catherine II]*

I beg Your Majesty to have confidence in me and to have the sentries removed from the second room, as the one I occupy is so small that I can hardly move in it. As Your Majesty knows I always stride about the room and my legs will swell if I cannot do so. Also I beg you to order that no officers should remain in the same room with me, as I have needs that I cannot possibly indulge in front of them. I beg Your Majesty not to treat me as a criminal as I have never offended Your Majesty. I recommend myself to Your Majesty's magnanimity and beg to be reunited with the indicated persons in Germany as soon as possible. God will repay Your Majesty.

Your very humble servant,<br>PETER.

P. S. Your Majesty may be sure that I will not undertake anything against her person or her reign.

YOUR MAJESTY,

If you do not wish to kill a man already sufficiently miserable, have pity on me and give me my only consolation which is Elisaveta Romanovna. It would be the greatest act of charity of your reign. If Your Majesty would grant me also the right to see Your Majesty for a moment I would be highly gratified.

Your humble servant,<br>PETER.

*[Written in Russian]*

YOUR MAJESTY,

Once again I beg you to let me, since I have followed your wishes in everything, leave for Germany with the persons for whom I have already asked Your Majesty to grant permission to accompany me. I hope Your Magnanimity will not permit my request to be in vain.

Your humble servant,

PETER.

— Reading No. 9 —

## CATHERINE II ANNOUNCES HER ACCESSION TO THE IMPERIAL THRONE

*By a quick stroke Catherine II, after assuring herself of the necessary military aid, deposed her husband, Peter III. Hereon events moved swiftly and successfully. Within a matter of a few days Peter died. According to Catherine's version, "fright had given him a colic" and "he gave up the ghost." On June 28, 1762, Catherine II was able triumphantly to announce "by the grace of God" her accession to the Imperial throne of Russia. (Cited by William Tooke,* Life of Catharine, *vol. 1, pp. 518-19, Philadelphia: William Fry, 1802.)*

✓　　　　✓　　　　✓

By the grace of God, Catharine II, empress and autocratrix of all the Russias, &c.

All true sons of Russia have clearly seen the great danger to which the whole Russian empire has actually been exposed. First, the foundations of our orthodox Greek religion have been shaken, and its traditions exposed to total destruction; so that there was absolutely reason to fear, that the faith which has been established in Russia from the earliest times, would be entirely changed, and foreign religion introduced. In the second place, the glory which Russia has acquired at the expense of so much blood, and which was carried to the highest pitch by her victorious arms, has been trampled under foot by the peace lately concluded with its most dangerous enemy. And lastly, the domestic regulations, which are the basis of the country's welfare, have been entirely overturned.

For these causes, overcome by the imminent perils with which our faithful subjects were threatened, and seeing how sincere and express their desires on this matter were: we, putting our trust in the Almighty and his divine justice, have ascended the sovereign imperial throne of all the Russians, and have received a solemn oath of fidelity from all our loving subjects.

*St. Petersburg, June 28, 1762.*

— Reading No. 10 —

# CZARTORYSKI ON THE EDUCATION OF ALEXANDER

*Aside from the prevailing ideas of the Age of Enlightenment, which undoubtedly had their impact upon Alexander, the education he received or failed to receive, according to Czartoryski, could explain his personality. (See Czartoryski, Memoirs, I, 127 ff., London: 1888.)*

↑       ↑       ↑

It is certainly astonishing that Catherine, who took pleasure in the thought that Alexander would continue her reign and her glory, did not think of preparing him for this task by familiarizing him in his early youth with the various branches of government. Nothing of the kind was attempted. Perhaps he would not have acquired very correct information on many things, but he would have been saved from the want of occupation. Yet it would seem that either the Empress and her council had no such idea, or that the former did not at least insist upon its being carried out. Alexander's education remained incomplete at the time of his marriage, in consequence of the departure of M. de la Harpe. He was then eighteen years old; he had no regular occupation, he was not even advised to work, and in the absence of any more practical task he was not given any plan of reading which might have helped him in the difficult career for which he was destined. I often spoke to him on this subject, both then and later. I proposed that he should read various books on history, legislation, and politics. He saw that they would do him good, and really wished to read them; but a Court life makes any continued occupation impossible. While he was Grand-Duke, Alexander did not read to the end a single serious book. I do not think he could have done so when he became Emperor, and the whole burden of a despotic government was cast upon him. The life of a Court is fatiguing and yet idle. It furnishes a thousand excuses for indolence, and one is constantly busy in doing nothing. When Alexander came to his rooms it was to take rest and not to work. He read by fits and starts, without ardour or zeal. The passion of acquiring knowledge was not sufficiently strong in him; he was married too young, and he did not perceive that he still knew very little. Yet he felt the importance of useful study, and wished to enter upon it; but his will was not sufficiently strong to overcome the daily obstacles presented by the duties and unpleasantness of life. The few years of his early youth thus passed away, and he lost precious opportunities which he had in abundance so long as Catherine was alive, and of which he might have recovered a part even under the Emperor Paul.

While he was Grand-Duke, and even during the first years of his reign, Alexander remained what his education had made him, and was very different from what he became later on when he followed his natural propensities. It must be concluded that nature had endowed him with rare qualities, as notwithstanding the education he had received he became the most amiable sovereign of his age and the cause of Napoleon's fall. After having reigned for some years, and acquired the experience entailed by the necessity of at once taking the management of important affairs of State and by constant intercourse with men in office, people were surprised to find him not a penetrating and subtle mind, writing without assistance excellent letters on complicated and difficult subjects, and always amiable, even in the most serious conversations. What would he have become had his education been less neglected and more adapted to the duties which were to occupy his life? M. de la Harpe was the only man that can be mentioned with praise among those to whom the education of the two Grand-Dukes was entrusted. I do not know exactly who were the persons directed by Catherine to select their tutors; probably they were some encyclopedists of the clique of Grimm or the Baron d'Holbach.

M. de la Harpe does not seem to have directed Alexander into any serious course of study, though he had acquired so much influence over the Grand-Duke's mind and heart that I believe he could make him do anything. Alexander derived from his teaching only some superficial knowledge; his information was neither positive nor complete. M. de la Harpe inspired him with the love of humanity, of justice, and even of equality and liberty for all; he prevented the prejudices and flatteries which surrounded him from stifling his noble instincts. It was a great merit in M. de la Harpe to have inspired and developed these generous sentiments in a Russian Grand-Duke, but Alexander's mind was not penetrated by them; it was filled with vague phrases, and M. de la Harpe did not sufficiently make him reflect on the immense difficulty of releasing these ideas—on the thorny task of finding means to obtain possible results. He was, however, merely charged with Alexander's literary education; the choice which was made of those who were to look after his moral training was extraordinary. . . .

# DOCUMENTS ON THE INTERREGNUM

*The sudden death of Alexander I caused a brief inter-regnum that caused the Decembrist revolt. Behind the two-week interregnum lies the simple cause that upon the news of the death of Alexander I, his brother Constantine, who was at the time in Warsaw, took an oath of loyalty to his brother Nicholas. His reason was that in 1822 he had abdicated the throne in favor of his younger brother Nicholas. The latter in the capital hastened to do likewise in favor of his elder brother Constantine, claiming that he was unaware of the act of abdication. Below are several documents that deal with this brief but important period. These included Constantine's request to abdicate and the consent expressed by his "affectionate brother Alexander" as well as an exchange of letters between Constantine and Nicholas during the period following the death of Alexander. (From* Readings in Russian History, *edited by Warren B. Walsh, third edition, 1959, pp. 257-58, 260-61, by permission of Syracuse University Press.)*

### Constantine to Alexander

Encouraged by all the proofs of the infinitely sympathetic disposition of your Imperial Majesty toward me I dare once more lay at your feet, Sire, a most humble prayer.

Not finding in myself the genius, the talents, nor the force necessary to be elevated to the Sovereign dignity to which I would have the right by my birth, I beg your Imperial Majesty to transfer this right to whom it would come after me, and thus to assure forever, the security of the empire. As to me, I will add by this renunciation a new guarantee and a new force to the engagement which I have voluntarily and solemnly contracted on the occasion of my divorce from my first wife.

All the circumstances of my own situation, bearing more and more upon this measure, prove to the Empire and to the entire world the sincerity of my sentiments.

Deign, Sire, to accept with good will my prayer; help me secure the consent of our Imperial Mother to this plan and sanction it with your Imperial assent.

In the sphere of private life, I shall pledge myself always to serve as an example to your faithful subjects, and to all those who are animated by a love for our dear country.

I am with a profound respect for your Majesty.

Your most faithful subject and brother<br>CONSTANTINE TSAREVICH

St. Petersburg
14/26 January, 1822.

*Alexander's reply*

VERY DEAR BROTHER: I have read your letter with all the attention that it merited. Having always fully appreciated the high sentiments of your heart, I found nothing in your letter to make me change my judgment. It has given me a new proof of your sincere attachment to the Empire, and of your solicitude for its continued tranquility.

In accordance with your desire I presented your letter to our beloved Mother; she has read it with the same recognition of the noble motives which guide you. Having taken into consideration the reason which you set forth, we both agree that you should be given full liberty to follow your immutable resolution, and we pray the All Powerful to bless the consequences of a purpose so pure.

I am ever your affectionate brother,

ALEXANDER

St. Petersburg,
2/14 February, 1822.

*Constantine to Nicholas*

VERY DEAR BROTHER: It is with an inexpressible affliction that I received at 7 o'clock in the evening the unhappy news of the death of our beloved Sovereign, of my benefactor, the Emperor Alexander.

. . . I ought to inform you that with this present letter I have addressed to her Imperial Majesty, our well beloved mother, a letter which announces to her, in virtue of an autograph receipt which I have received from the Emperor, on the second [fourteenth] of February, 1822, in response to a letter which I have written him renouncing succession to the Imperial throne, Mother, and honored by her assent which she has deigned to confirm to me, my irrevocable resolution to cede to you my rights to the succession to the Imperial throne of all the Russians.

. . . I am with the most profound veneration, Sire, of your Imperial Majesty, the most faithful subject,

CONSTANTINE

*Warsaw, 25 November/7 December 1825*

*Nicholas to Constantine*

MY DEAR CONSTANTINE: I bow before my sovereign, after having pronounced together with those persons who found themselves before me, the oath which is due him. . . . In the name of heaven do not abandon us, and do not desert us!

Your brother and your faithful subject in life and in death,

NICHOLAS

*27 November/9 December 1825*

*Constantine to Nicholas*

Your Aid de camp, my dear Nicholas, has just given me your letter. I have read it with the most vivid chagrin. My decision, sanctified by him who was my benefactor and my Sovereign, is irrevocable. I am not able to accept your proposal to hasten my departure for St. Petersburg, and I warn you that I shall leave Warsaw only to retire to some greater distance, if everything is not arranged following the will of our deceased Emperor.

Your faithful brother and sincere friend,<br>CONSTANTINE

*Warsaw, 6/18 December*

### EDICT OF NICHOLAS

By the grace of God, we, Nicholas, Emperor and Autocrat of all the Russians, etc. make known to all our faithful subjects:

. . . . . . . . .

In consequence of all these acts, and after the fundamental law of the Empire on the order of succession, with a heart full of respect for the impenetrable decrees of Providence who leads us, We ascended the throne of our ancestors, the throne of the empire of all the Russians, and those of the kingdom of Poland and the Grand Duchy of Finland which are inseparable, and we order:

1. That the oath of fidelity be taken to us and to our heir, His Imperial Highness Alexander, our well beloved son;

2. That the epoch of our accession to the throne shall be dated from the 19th November 1825. [O.S.]

. . . . . . . . .

Given in our imperial residence of St. Petersburg, the 12th/24th of December in the years of grace, 1825 and of our reign first.

NICHOLAS

## — Reading No. 12 —

# OPEN LETTER OF THE REVOLUTIONARY EXECUTIVE COMMITTEE TO THE NEW SOVEREIGN, ALEXANDER III

*Shortly after the assassination of Alexander II the Revolutionary Executive Committee addressed an Open Letter to the new sovereign, Alexander III. After explaining to him the reason for his father's tragic end, the Committee put down two conditions that might end po-*

*litical terror and restore peace and public order. A part
of the letter follows. The complete text of this historical
document is quoted by George F. Kennan,* Siberia and
the Exile System, *vol. II, pp. 499-503, London: 1891.*

✓         ✓         ✓

March 10, 1881

YOUR MAJESTY: Although the Executive Committee
understands fully the grievous oppression that you must
experience at this moment, it believes that it has no right
to yield to the feeling of natural delicacy which would
perhaps dictate the postponement of the following explanation to another time. There is something higher
than the most legitimate human feeling, and that is duty
to one's country—the duty for which a citizen must
sacrifice himself and his own feelings, and even the feelings of others. In obedience to this all-powerful duty we
have decided to address you at once, waiting for nothing,
as will wait for nothing the historical process that threatens us with rivers of blood and the most terrible con-
vulsions.

The tragedy enacted on the Ekaterinski canal [location
of the assassination of Alexander II] was not a mere
casualty, nor was it unexpected. After all that had happened in the course of the previous decade it was absolutely inevitable. . . .

We address your Majesty as those who have discarded
all prejudices, and who have suppressed the distrust
created by the actions of the Government throughout a
century. We forget that you are the representative of the
authority that has so often deceived and that has so injured
the people. We address you as a citizen and and as an honest man. We hope that the feeling of personal exasperation will extinguish in your mind your consciousness of
your duties and your desire to know the truth. We also
might feel exasperation. You have lost your father. We
have lost not only our father, but our brothers, our wives,
our children and our dearest friends. But we are ready
to suppress personal feeling if it be demanded by the
welfare of Russia. We expect the same from you.

We set no conditions for you—do not let our pro-
position irritate you. The conditions that are prerequisite
to a change from revolutionary activity to peaceful labor

are created, not by us, but by history. These conditions, in our opinion, are two.

1. A general amnesty to cover all past political crimes; for the reason that they were not crimes but fulfillments of civil duty.

2. The summoning of representatives of the whole Russian people to examine the existing framework of social and governmental life, and to remodel it in accordance with the people's wishes.

We regard it as necessary, however, to remind you that the legalization of the Supreme Power, by the representatives of the people, can be valid only in case the elections are perfectly free. For this reason such elections must be held under the following conditions.

1. Delegates are to be sent from all classes, without distinction, and in number are to be proportionate to the number of inhabitants.

2. There shall be no limitations, either for voters or delegates.

3. The canvass and the elections shall be absolutely unrestricted, and therefore the Government, pending the organization of the National Assembly, shall authorize, in the form of temporary measures,

    a. Complete freedom of the press.
    b. Complete freedom of speech.
    c. Complete freedom of public meeting.
    d. Complete freedom of election program.

This is the only way in which Russia can return to the part of normal and peaceful development.

We declare solemnly, before the people of our native land and before the whole world, that our part will submit unconditionally to the decisions of a National Assembly elected in the manner above indicated, and that we will not allow ourselves, in future, to offer violent resistance to any Government that the National Assembly may sanction.

And now, your Majesty, decide! Before you are two courses, and you are to make your choice between them. We can only trust that your intelligence and conscience may suggest to you the only decision that is compatible with the welfare of Russia, with your own dignity, and with your duty to your native land.

THE EXECUTIVE COMMITTEE

## — Reading No. 13 —

# SAMSON-HIMMERLSTIERNA'S SKETCH OF ALEXANDER III

*The following sketch of Alexander III comes from the work of H. von Samson-Himmerlstierna. The author, an East Prussian, had nothing but contempt for Russia and the Russian people. Whatever lay east of Germany the author regarded with the arrogance of a Prussian Junker. Curiously enough, the profiles of and the comparisons between Nicholas I and his grandson Alexander III, sovereigns of Imperial Russia, reveal an unusually keen discernment on the part of the author; he sensed the importance of the period in the history of the Russian Empire—the swan song of autocracy. (From* Russia Under Alexander III, *pp. 12 ff., tr. by J. Morrison, New York: Macmillan, 1893.)*

✐          ✐          ✐

Alexander III's repugnance to the Western European system is closely bound up with this inner instability of his nature. It is in part founded upon the wish of the Emperor, at least in this one point, to possess a bond of union with the instinct of the people, and a reserve power in case of need, but more especially upon the thought that the Western development is, in his eyes, an uncanny and incommensurable quantity, which must be introduced as little as possible, and reckoned with as quickly as possible. The peculiarities so often mentioned in the daily life of the Tsar are explained by this contradiction between his own real nature and the nature of his duties, which excludes all dependence on others. He prefers to transact business with his ministers and generals rather by writing than by word of mouth, as he wishes to avoid the discussion of subjects with which he is unacquainted. As a matter of duty he receives hundreds of his subjects from all parts of his enormous Empire; but he never allows them to discuss minute points, because he fears explanations which may lead to difficulties. He avoids as far as possible direct and lengthy transactions with foreign diplomatists, because he has no confidence in his power of estimating them at their proper value, and because he has less facility in expressing himself in French than he would like to avow. Conscientious and industrious, he has gradually learnt to master the little round of his official duties: what lies outside this is carefully avoided, and for this reason meetings and intercourse with foreign monarchs are limited to the utmost (his friendly and unpretentious father-in-law naturally excepted). The fear of being forced to play a second part follows the grandson of the "infallible" Nicholas like a phantom. As is natural, the depression of the Tsar, who is constantly preoccupied in fulfilling the duties of his position, communicates itself to his *entourage,* and this depression produces a feeling of discomfort in the life of the Court which cannot be disputed by the most friendly witnesses. Although personally courageous he feels the prudential considerations that have to be taken with regard to the thousand dangers that surround him so galling as to deprive life of all its joy. Crushed by his official position, and compelled to constant repression of his true nature, he rises above the contradiction between *being* and *seeming* most of all during those periodical visits which he makes to the Court of Denmark. Here, where the feeling of responsibility is cast aside, he can give free play to his frank, pleasant, robust nature, but in the ordinary course of things he represses his feelings with a painful conscientiousness. Still the inner discord betrays itself to the attentive observer everywhere—in the salon, on parade, and even in the midst of festivities. The appearance of the tall, stately, vigorous man with the fine broad forehead betokens a mixture of strength and weakness, disdainful pride and invincible shyness, a mind constantly occupied with itself. This explains how he, who as a prince was merely unsociable, has arrived at a degree of isolation within the last few years which surpasses anything ever shown by his predecessors.

## — Reading No. 14 —

# NICHOLAS II ADDRESSES THE NOBILITY AND THE ZEMTSVOS, 1895

*The accession of Nicholas II in 1894 caused nationwide speculation about his political tendencies. It was not long before the new Emperor revealed his ideas. On January 29, 1895, as a gesture of courtesy, representatives of the nobility and of the zemstvos were received by Nicholas II. During the official ceremony the young Emperor read a brief address, believed to have been written by K. P. Pobedonostsev, former tutor and counselor. The speech carried with it enormous political significance: it advised all the hopeful subjects to abandon their "senseless dreams" for the Emperor planned to follow the footsteps of his late father Alexander III. Cited below are the address of Nicholas II and the reply he received in the form of an "Open Letter." (From P. N. Miliukov, Russia and Its Crisis, Chicago: University of Chicago Press, 1905, pp. 327-28.)*

✦    ✦    ✦

"I am pleased to see here the representatives of all classes assembled to express their feeling of loyalty. I believe in the sincerity of those sentiments which have always been characteristic of every Russian. But I am aware that in certain meetings of the Zemstvos voices have lately been raised by persons carried away by senseless dreams as to the participation of the Zemstvo representatives in matters of internal government. Let all know that, in devoting all my strength to the welfare of the people, I intend to protect the principle of autocracy as firmly and unswervingly as did my late and never-to-be-forgotten father."

*To this the liberals replied in an "Open Letter" thus:*

"You have told your mind, and your words will be known to all Russia, to all the civilized world. Until now nobody knew you; since yesterday you became a 'definite quantity,' and 'senseless dreams' are no longer possible on your account. We do not know whether you clearly understand the situation created by your 'firm' utterance. But people who do not stand so high above and so far off from actuality can easily comprehend what is their own and your position concerning what is now the state of things in Russia. First of all, you are imperfectly informed. No zemstvoist has put the question as you put it, and no voice was raised in any Zemstvo assembly against autocracy. . . . The question was only to remove the wall of bureaucracy and court influences which separate the Tsar from Russia; and these were the tendencies which you in your inexperience and lack of knowledge ventured to stamp as 'senseless dreams.' . . . Unhappily, your unfortunate expression is not a mere slip of language, not an occasional lapse; it reflects a deliberate system. Russian society realized very well that not an ideal autocrat has spoken to them January 29, but a bureaucracy jealous of its omnipotence. . . . January 29 has dispelled that halo which surrounded your young, uncertain appearance in the eyes of many Russians. You yourself raised your hands against your own popularity. But not your popularity alone is now at stake. If autocracy in word and deed proclaims itself identical with the omnipotence of bureaucracy, if it can exist only so long as society is voiceless it is lost. It digs its own grave, and soon or late—at any rate, in a future not very remote—it will fall beneath the pressure of living social forces. . . . The alternative you put before the society is such that the mere fact of its being clearly formulated and openly proclaimed implies a terrible threat to autocracy. You challenged the Zemstvos, and with them Russian society, and nothing remains for them now but to choose between progress and faithfulness to autocracy. Your speech has provoked a feeling of offense and depression; but the living social forces will soon recover from that feeling. Some of them will pass to a peaceful but systematic and conscious struggle for such scope of

action as is necessary for them. Some others will be
made more determined to fight the detestable regime by
any means. You first began the struggle; and the struggle
will come."

— Reading No. 15 —

# ALEXANDER KERENSKY ON NICHOLAS II

*Member of the Third and Fourth Dumas, leader of the
Laborite opposition in the Duma, Vice-Chairman of the
Petrograd Soviet, Minister of Justice, Minister of War
and Navy, and finally, Prime Minister in the Provisional
Government, such is the career of Alexander F. Kerensky.
Crucifixion of Liberty is the author's account of his experiences and an attempt to explain the failure of the
provisional government. Throughout this work the reader
will find lively sketches of historical figures among which
is the characterization of Nicholas II cited below. (Reprinted from Crucifixion of Liberty, by Alexander Karen-
sky, New York, by permission of The John Day Company, Inc., 1934, p. 173.)*

There was always this mystery about Nicholas II: why,
having been born to rule strictly as a constitutional monarchy—to reign but not to rule—did he hate the very
word "constitution" so much and refuse to let the burden
of absolute rule slip out of his wavering hands, for
which it was all too heavy? "Be as Peter the Great was"
drummed the Empress into him. But to great Peter his
autocratic powers were a mighty instrument of statesmanship: he ruled in order to build a great empire. Nicholas
II made no attempt to build, he merely defended his

powers, burdensome as they were to him, against internal foes. I do not think he knew the reason himself. He merely believed what his father and Pobiedonostsev had instilled into him: there could be no Russia without autocracy; Russia and the autocracy were one; he himself was the impersonation of the autocracy. So the magic circle closed. There was no way out, unless it was one into disaster and void. Perhaps the very reason why he took his enforced abdication so calmly was that he saw in it divine help, a relief from the burden of power which he could not throw off of his own accord because he was bound by his oath as "The Lord's annointed." Living in the twentieth century, he had the mentality of the Muscovite Kings, even though he had no blood connection with the Moscow dynasty. The daily work of a monarch he found intolerably boring. He could not stand listening long or seriously to ministers' reports, or reading them. He liked such ministers as could tell an amusing story and did not weary the monarch's attention with too much business. But I repeat that never—from the very beginning to the very end of his reign—did he willingly yield one inch of his autocracy. When it came to defending his divine right his usual indifference left him; he became cunning, obstinate and cruel, merciless at times.

— Reading No. 16 —

# EXTRACT FROM AN ADDRESS OF THE MINISTER TO THE TSAR

.   .   .   .   .   .   .   .   .   .   .

Yesterday, at the meeting of the Council of Ministers under Your personal chairmanship, we laid before You our unanimous appeal that Grand Duke Nicholas Nicholaevich should not be removed from his part in the supreme command of the army. But we fear that Your

Imperial Majesty did not deign to incline to our plea, which, in our opinion, is the plea of all loyal Russia.

Sire, we dare once more to tell You that, to the best of our understanding, Your decision threatens Russia, Yourself, and Your dynasty with evil consequences. . . .

*Sept. 3, 1915*                    [Signed by eight ministers]

— Reading No. 17 —

# EXTRACT FROM A LETTER OF THE EMPRESS TO NICHOLAS II

*The numerous letters of the Empress to her "hubby" indicate the evil influence which she had exerted upon her weak husband. Her constant reminding to Nicholas II of the "real enemies" and of those "who would do harm to the people" were bound to carry their effect in the end. The result was the hesitance, the frequent shift in government, ministerial, and military appointments, and blunderings leading to deeper crises. Here is only one instance—part of a letter of the Empress to Nicholas II.*

✓              ✓              ✓

September 4, 1915

.    .    .    .    .    .    .    .    .

Tell me the impression, if you can. Be firm to the end, let me be sure of that otherwise shall get quite ill from anxiety.

Bitter pain not to be with you—know what you feel, and the meeting with N. won't be agreeable—you did trust him and now you know, what months ago our Friend [Rasputin] said, that he was acting wrongly towards you and your country and wife—its not the people who would do harm to your people but Nikolasha and get Guchkov, Rodzianko, Samarin, etc. . . .

## — Reading No. 18 —

# PURISHKEVICH DESCRIBES THE PLOT AGAINST RASPUTIN

*V. M. Purishkevich was the leader of the extreme Right party in the Second, Third, and Fourth Dumas. A monarchist who staunchly defended absolutism on every occasion, he became alarmed by the course of events during the war years, particularly by the influence which Rasputin came to exert upon the Court as well as upon national affairs. Motivated exclusively by a desire to save the monarchy, Purishkevich decided to join a small group of plotters who schemed to rid the country of that evil man. Following are some excerpts from the Diary of Purishkevich, describing the origin of the plot. (From V. Pourichkevitch, "Comment J'ai Tué Raspoutine." Cited by Frank Golder, Documents on Russian History, pp. 175-76, New York: The Century Co., 1927.)*

✐          ✐          ✐

December 2, 1916

For the first time in many years I have had the moral satisfaction to feel that I have done my duty honestly, conscientiously, and courageously. I made a speech in the Duma on the present state of Russia. I addressed myself to the Government, demanding that the truth be laid bare before the Emperor, who is surrounded by clever intriguers. I demanded that the Monarch be warned against the danger that threatens Russia from the obscure forces in the rear.

Today, for the first time, I have gone back on my oath—oath of silence. I did it not for political reasons, not for the sake of gaining the good-will of the militant members of the hostile political parties, but in order that the voice of the Russian people might reach the throne.

\*      \*      \*

I expressed the thoughts of thousands of the best Russians, regardless of political parties and opinions. I felt that I had done so as I left the Duma platform after having spoken for two hours. I felt it in the shouts of "Bravo;" in the clapping of hands, in the faces of the excited crowd which gathered around me after my speech. Among them were representatives of Russian society; for on this day the Taurida Palace was filled with the intellectual and social leaders of the nation and its highest functionaries.

I know that I have expressed the feeling of Russia. I know that there was not a single false note in my speech. . . .

December 3

I have not had a moment's peace today. As I sat at my desk I have been kept busy answering the telephone, which has not stopped ringing for a second. From morning until evening all kinds of people, known and unknown, call up to congratulate me. I must confess that it has reached a point where I can no longer remain at my desk. It is difficult to imagine a situation more stupid than the one I am in, sitting listening to these nightingales singing my praise without being able to stop them.

\*      \*      \*

Among those who telephoned was a Prince Iusupov [Youssoupoff], Count Sumarokov-Elston. He has aroused my curiosity. After expressing the usual compliments he inquired if he could see me to explain certain things about Rasputin's relation with the Court, things which he could not tell over the telephone. I made an appointment for tomorrow morning at nine. I am anxious to know what he has to say and what he wants.

December 4

He was on time . . . and at once made a very good impression on me. . . . He looks as if he possessed a great deal of will power and much strength of character. . . .

"Your speech will not have the results you expect," said he. "The Emperor does not like to have one bring pressure on him. Rasputin's power will grow greater rather than less owing to his boundless influence over the Empress. It is she who really governs the State. The Emperor is at Headquarters much occupied with military operations."

"Well, what are we going to do about it?" I asked.

He gave a mysterious smile and looked me straight in the face.

"Get rid of Rasputin."

"That's easy to say. But who will do it? Russia has nobody with backbone enough for such a deed. The Government could do it easily, but the Government clings to him and watches over him as if he were a treasure."

"Yes," said Iusupov, "one can not count on the Government, but I dare say there are men in Russia who would do it. . . ."

I smiled. "Prince," said I to him, "I am no longer astonished at anything that happens in Russia. I am not trying to get anything for myself; I have no personal ambitions. But if you wish . . . to deliver Russia from Rasputin, here is my hand. We are going to examine the means to bring it about, and we will undertake it if we can find some others to join us. . . ."

— Reading No. 19 —

# PRINCE YOUSSOUPOFF ON RASPUTIN

*Prince Felix Youssoupoff was an active organizer and participant of the plot to assassinate Rasputin. The assassination was carried out in his palatial place in Petrograd. Prince Youssoupoff was assisted by V. Purishkevich and a few others. Youssoupoff's recent book,* Lost Splendor, *contains an explanation as to why the "malignant influ-*

*ence of the old lewd man" was so strong and his prestige
so great. (From Prince Felix Youssoupoff, Lost Splendor,
New York: Putnam, 1954, pp. 195, 197.*

✓　　　　　✓　　　　　✓

There is no doubt that the staretz [Rasputin] possessed
hypnotic powers. Stolypin, the Minister of the Interior,
who waged a determined war against him, tells how
Rasputin, when he had been sent for, attempted to hypno-
tize him:

"He ran his colourless eyes over me, muttering mysterious and incoherent passages from the Bible, and
making strange passes in the air with his hands. I was
conscious of a growing feeling of intense antagonism and
repulsion for the scoundrel who sat facing me; he was
just beginning to gain an ascendancy over me when I
managed to regain control over myself and, cutting him
short, bluntly told him that he was completely in my
power."

Stolypin was assassinated a few months after this inter-
view; he had already had a narrow escape when an attempt was made on his life in 1906.

Rasputin's scandalous behaviour, his occult influence
over the Imperial couple, his obscene morals, stirred the
indignation of the more clear-sighted people in St. Petersburg. The press itself, braving the censor, denounced the
"staretz's" infamous conduct.

Rasputin thought it would be wise to make himself
scarce, for a time at least. In March 1911 he seized his
pilgrim's staff and left for Jerusalem, and thence for
Tsaritsine where he spent the summer with one of his
cronies, a monk by the name of Héliodore. When he
came back at the beginning of the following winter, he
resumed his dissolute life.

. . . During the autumn of 1912, while the Imperial
family was staying at Spala, in Poland, an apparently
slight accident caused a terrible attack of haemophilia
which endangered the Tsarevitch's life. Priests prayed
night and day in the church at Spala; a service was held
in Moscow before the miraculous ikon of the Blessed
Virgin of Iversakaia; in St. Petersburg the people prayed
incessantly at the Cathedral of Our Lady of Kazan. Rasputin, who was in constant touch with Spala, telegraphed

the Tsarina: "God has seen your tears and heard your prayers. Do not grieve: your son will live." The next day the child's temperature went down; two days later he was out of danger, and the poor Tsarina's faith in the "holy man" was naturally intensified.

— Reading No. 20 —

# TEXT OF NICHOLAS II'S ABDICATION

*On March 15, 1917, Nicholas II was approached by two members of the Duma, who were secretly dispatched to the military headquarters with a suggestion that the Tsar abdicate the throne. The purpose of the request, it may be noted, was to save rather than destroy the monarchy. Nicholas hesitated, believing at first, as did others, that he abdicated in favor of his son Alexis. But the haemophilic condition of the tsarevich barred such action. After several hours of wavering, Nicholas II, on March 15, 1917, shortly before midnight, officially abdicated on behalf of himself as well as his son in favor of his brother, Grand Duke Michael. The text of the abdication act follows:*

✓          ✓          ✓

We, Nicholas II, by the Grace of God Emperor of Russia, Tsar of Poland, Grand Duke of Finland, &c., &c., declare to all our faithful subjects:

"In the days of a great struggle against an external enemy who for three years has been striving to enslave our country, it has pleased the Lord God to send down on Russia new and severe trials. The internal tumults which have begun threaten to have a fatal effect on the further progress of this obstinate war. The destiny of

Russia, the honour of our heroic army, the welfare of the people, and the whole future of our dear fatherland demand that the war shall be conducted at all costs to a victorious end. A cruel foe is exerting his last strength, and the hour is already near when our valiant army, in concert with our glorious Allies, will finally overthrow the enemy.

"In these decisive days in the life of Russia we have considered it our duty to make it easier for our people to unite and organize all their forces for the swift attainment of victory, and in agreement with the Imperial Duma we have decided for the good of the country to abdicate the throne of Russia and lay down the supreme power.

"Not wishing to part from our beloved son, we bequeath the heritage to our brother, the Grand Duke Michael Alexandrovich. Blessing him on his accession to the throne, we adjure our brother to rule in affairs of State in full and unbroken harmony with the representatives of the people in the legislative institutions, on principles which they determine, and to take an inviolable oath to this effect, in the name of our dearly beloved country.

"We call upon all faithful sons of the fatherland to fulfil their sacred duty to it by obeying the *tsar* in this grave time of national trial, and to help him, along with the representatives of the people, to lead the Russian State on the path of victory, prosperity, and glory.

"May the Lord God help Russia."

(Signed) NICHOLAS

## — Reading No. 21 —

# THE GRAND DUKE MICHAEL'S MANIFESTO, MARCH 16, 1917

*The abdication of Nicholas II in favor of his brother, Grand Duke Michael, placed the latter in a most difficult position. After he had given most serious consideration as to what course to choose, Grand Duke Michael publicly consented to accept the throne provided his candidacy was approved by a Constitutent Assembly selected by universal, direct, equal, and secret ballot. For all practical purposes by this act the Romanov dynasty ended. The gates to the revolution were now wide open. Following is the Manifesto as proclaimed by Grand Duke Michael on March 16, 1917:*

"A heavy burden has been laid upon me by the will of my brother, who in a time of unexampled strife and popular tumult has transferred to me the imperial throne of Russia. Sharing with the people the thought that the good of the country should stand before everything else, I have firmly decided that I will accept power only if that is the will of our great people, who must by universal suffrage elect their representatives to a Constituent Assembly, in order to determine the form of government and draw up new fundamental laws for Russia. Therefore, calling for the blessing of God, I ask all citizens of Russia to obey the Provisional Government, which has arisen and been endowed with full authority on the initiative of the Imperial Duma, until such time as the Constituent Assembly, called at the earliest possible date and elected on the basis of universal, direct, equal, and secret suffrage, shall by its decision as to the form of government give expression to the will of the people."

# — Reading No. 22 —

# TROTSKY ON THE END OF THE ROYAL FAMILY AT EKATERINBURG

*The royal family, after being banished from the capital to Tobolsk was later sent back to Ekaterinburg. When the latter city came under danger of being taken over by the rebellious Czech Legion the local Soviet authorities made the terse announcement that because it was feared that with the aid of the approaching enemy the imprisoned royal family might escape, "the Presidium of the Regional Soviet . . . had decided that the former Tsar Nicholas, Nicholas Romanov . . . is to be shot." During the night of July 16-17, 1918, the sentence was carried out. With Nicholas II perished the entire family. The bodies were cremated and never found; for this reason various stories have arisen as to the actual fate of the Romanov family. Following is an excerpt concerning the event from Leon Trotsky's Diary. (Reprinted by permission of the publishers from* Trotsky's Diary In Exile, *translated from the Russian by Elena Zarudnaya, Cambridge, Mass.: Harvard University Press, Copyright, 1958, by The President and Fellows of Harvard College.)*

✓      ✓      ✓

April 9

The White press at one time hotly debated the question of who it was that ordered the execution of the Tsar's family. The liberals, it seemed, inclined to the opinion that the Ural Executive Committee, being cut off from Moscow, had acted independently. That is not correct. The resolution was adopted in Moscow. The affair took place during a very critical period of the Civil War, when I was spending almost all my time at the front, and my recollections about the case of the Tsar's family are rather fragmentary. I shall relate here what I remember.

During one of my short visits to Moscow—I think a few weeks before the execution of the Romanovs—I incidentally mentioned in the Politburo that, considering the bad situation in the Urals, it would be expedient to accelerate the Tsar's trial. I proposed that we hold an open court trial which would reveal a picture of the whole reign, with its peasant policy, labor policy, national minority and cultural policies, its two wars, etc. The proceedings of the trial would be broadcast throughout the country by radio; (?) [*the question mark is written in above the line*] in the *volosts* [districts including several villages], accounts of the proceedings would be read and commented upon every day. Lenin replied to the effect that it would be very good if it were feasible. But . . . there might not be enough time. . . . No debate took place, since I did not insist on my proposal, being absorbed in other work. And in the Politburo, as I remember, there were just three or four of us: Lenin, myself, Sverdlov . . . Kamenev, as I recall, was not there. At that period Lenin was in a rather gloomy mood and did not feel very confident that we would succeed in building an army. . . . My next visit to Moscow took place after the fall of Ekaterinburg. Talking to Sverdlov, I asked in passing: "Oh yes, and where is the Tsar?" "It's all over," he answered, "He has been shot." "And where is the family?" "And the family along with him." "All of them?" I asked, apparently with a touch of surprise. "All of them!" replied Sverdlov, "What about it?" He was waiting to see my reaction. I made no reply. "And who made the decision?" I asked. "We decided it here. Ilyich believed that we shouldn't leave the Whites a live banner to rally around, especially under the present difficult circumstances. . . ." I did not ask any further questions, and considered the matter closed. Actually, the decision was not only expedient but necessary. The severity of this summary justice showed the world that we would continue to fight on mercilessly, stopping at nothing. The execution of the Tsar's family was needed not only in order to frighten, horrify, and dishearten the enemy, but also in order to shake up our own ranks, to show them that there was no turning back, that ahead lay either complete victory or complete ruin. In the intellectual circles of the Party there probably were misgivings and shakings of heads. But the masses of workers and soldiers had not a minute's doubt. They would not have understood and would not have accepted any other decision. *This* Lenin sensed well. The ability to think and feel for and with the masses was characteristic of him to the highest degree, especially at the great political turning points. . . .

When I was abroad I read *Poslednie Novosti* a description of the shooting, the burning of the bodies, etc. How much of all this is true and how much is invented, I have not the least idea, since I was never curious about *how* the sentence was carried out and, frankly, do not understand such curiosity.

# A SELECTED BIBLIOGRAPHY

Bain, R. N., *The Daughter of Peter the Great,* New York: E. P. Dutton & Co., 1900.

Bain, R. N., *Slavonic Europe. A Political History of Poland and Russia from 1447 to 1796,* New York: Cambridge University Press, 1906.

Collyer, A. D. (ed.), *The Despatches and Correspondence of John, Second Earl of Buckinghamshire, Ambassador to the Court of Catherine II, 1762-1765,* London: Longmans, Green & Co. 1900-01. 2 vols.

Florinsky, M. T., *Russia. A History and an Interpretation,* New York: The Macmillan Co., 1953. 2 vols.

Gielgud, Adam (ed.), *Memoirs of Prince Adam Czartoryski and his Correspondence with Alexander I,* London: 1888. 2 vols.

Golder, Frank A., *Documents of Russian History, 1914-17,* New York: The Century Co., 1927.

Gurko, V. I., *Features and Figures of the Past. Government and Opinion in the Reign of Nicholas II,* Stanford University Press, 1939.

Kennan, George, *Siberia and the Exile System,* London: James R. Osgood, McIlvaine & Co., 1891, 2 vols.

Kerensky, Alexander F., *The Crucifixion of Liberty,* New York: John Day Co., 1934.

Klyuchevsky, V. O., *A History of Russia,* New York: Dutton, 1911-1931. 5 vols.

Kokovtsov, V. N., *Out of My Past,* Stanford University Press, 1935. *Letters of the Tsar to the Tsaritsa, 1914-1917.* Tr. by A. L. Hynes, London-New York: Dodd, Mead & Co., 1929.

de Manstein, C. H., *Memoirs of Russia, Historical, Political, and Military, from 1727 to 1744,* London: 1770.

Mazour, Anatole G., *The First Russian Revolution, 1825,* Berkeley: University of California Press, 1937.

*Memoirs of Catherine the Great,* Ed. by Dominique Meroger, with an introduction by G. P. Gooch; New York: The Macmillan Co., n.d.

Miliukov, Paul, *Russia and Its Crisis,* Chicago: Chicago University Press, 1905.

Mirsky, D. S., *Russia; A Social History,* London: Benn, 1927.

Pares, Bernard, *The Fall of the Russian Monarchy. A Study of the Evidence,* New York: Alfred A. Knopf, 1939.

184

Samson-Himmelstierna, H. Von, *Russia Under Alexander III,*
    Tr. by J. Morrison, Ed. by Felix Volkhovsky; New York:
    Macmillan & Co., 1893.

Schuyler, Eugene, *Peter the Great,* New York: Charles Scrib-
    ner's Sons, 1884. 2 vols.

Seton-Watson, Hugh, *The Decline of Imperial Russia, 1854-
    1914,* London: Methuen & Co., 1952.

Strakhovsky, L. I., *Alexander I of Russia,* New York: W. W.
    Norton & Co., Inc., 1947.

Walsh, Warren B., (Compiled and edited) *Readings in Rus-
    sian History,* Syracuse University Press, 1948.

Youssoupoff, Prince Felix, *Lost Splendor,* New York: G. P.
    Putnam's Sons, 1954.

# INDEX

No. 1    MA... ...CH MIND
         By ...

No. 2    THE ... Short His-
         to...

No. 3    THE ... History
         By Herman Ausubel

No. 4    THE WORLD IN THE TWENTIETH CENTURY
         By Louis L. Snyder

No. 5    50 MAJOR DOCUMENTS OF THE TWENTIETH
         CENTURY—By Louis L. Snyder

No. 6    THE AGE OF REASON—By Louis L. Snyder

No. 7    MARX AND THE MARXISTS: The Ambiguous
         Legacy—By Sidney Hook

No. 8    NATIONALISM: Its Meaning and History
         By Hans Kohn

No. 9    MODERN JAPAN: A Brief History
         By Arthur Tiedemann

No. 10   50 MAJOR DOCUMENTS OF THE NINE-
         TEENTH CENTURY—By Louis L. Snyder

No. 11   CONSERVATISM: From John Adams to Churchill
         By Peter Viereck

No. 12   THE PAPACY: A Brief History
         By James A. Corbett

No. 13   THE AGE OF THE REFORMATION
         By Roland H. Bainton

No. 14   BASIC DOCUMENTS IN AMERICAN HISTORY
         By Richard B. Morris

No. 15   CONTEMPORARY AFRICA: Continent in Tran-
         sition—By T. Walter Wallbank

No. 16   THE RUSSIAN REVOLUTIONS OF 1917
         By John Shelton Curtiss

No. 17   THE GREEK MIND—By Walter R. Agard

No. 18   BRITISH CONSTITUTIONAL HISTORY SINCE
         1832—By Robert Livingston Schuyler and Co-
         rinne Comstock Weston

No. 19   THE NEGRO IN THE UNITED STATES: A
         Brief History—By Rayford W. Logan

No. 20   AMERICAN CAPITALISM: Its Promise and Ac-
         complishment—By Louis M. Hacker

No. 21   LIBERALISM—By J. Salwyn Schapiro

No. 22   THE ERA OF THE FRENCH REVOLUTION,
         1789-1799: Ten Years That Shook the World
         By Leo Gershoy

No. 23   BASIC HISTORY OF MODERN GERMANY
         By Louis L. Snyder

No. 24   BASIC HISTORY OF MODERN RUSSIA: Politi-
         cal, Cultural and Social Trends—By Hans Kohn